Twice Upon a Time

Twice Upon a Time

by

DONALD D. McCALL

❧ ❧ ❧
❧ ❧ ❧
❧ ❧ ❧

MOODY PRESS
CHICAGO

To Karen

© 1971 by
THE MOODY BIBLE INSTITUTE
OF CHICAGO

Library of Congress Catalog Card Number: 75-143475

Printed in the United States of America

CONTENTS

ACKNOWLEDGMENTS

I want to extend my thanks to the women of the Synodical of Minnesota whose invitations to speak at their annual meetings occasioned the assembling of these chapters, to three congregations who have in steadfast love encouraged me in the preaching of the gospel, and to Miss Jean Howard for the typing and retyping of these many pages.

INTRODUCTION

WHEN ELIHU ATTEMPTED to reason with Job to convince him that he ought not to strive against God, he opened his argument with the statement, "God speaketh once, yea twice, yet man perceiveth it not" (Job 33:14). This one sentence standing alone may be seen as a summary of the whole history of God's speaking to man. God speaks in one way and then another. Thus it is always the task of the church to help man in every generation to understand the meaning of God's Word. The human spirit possessed with the Word of God has always reached out for some method of expressing that Word, whether it be through parables, fables, allegories, or aphorisms. This need to communicate the gospel is the constant challenge of the classroom, the primary purpose of the pulpit, and a real responsibility of parents in the nurturing of Christian discipleship in their children.

One of the most popular means of instruction since primitive times has been the use of short stories such as fables and the "once upon a time" stories. This means of imparting instruction for the proper conduct of life is both dramatic and effective. Consequently, almost all cultures have a body of literary fables which have existed for centuries.

7

The most familiar fables today are those of Aesop, which originated in the centuries before Christ when Greece was the dominant civilization upon the face of the earth. These fictitious tales designed to illustrate some maxim of conduct or some truth of life might today be used to illustrate nobler thoughts. That, in fact, is the purpose and intent of this book: that the familiar fables of Aesop might be used as introductions to passages in the Word of God; that we might project the *ideas* of the fables into the *ideals* of biblical thought.

Truly, God spoke "once upon a time," yes, even "twice upon a time," and the wonder of it all is that we may still perceive new meanings in that Word once spoken for all mankind!

THE HARE AND THE TORTOISE

Once upon a time there was a hare who was always making fun of a tortoise for being so slow. "Do you ever get anywhere?" asked the hare with a sarcastic laugh.

"Yes," replied the patient tortoise, "and I get there sooner than you think."

"No one can run faster than I," bragged the hare. "I will challenge anyone here to run a race with me."

To the hare's surprise the tortoise accepted the challenge. Though the hare was greatly amused at the thought of running a race with a tortoise, still, for the fun of it all, he agreed.

The fox who had consented to serve as judge had marked off a course to the woods and back again.

The race began and soon the hare was far out of sight. Then, to make the tortoise see how ridiculous it was for him to even try to race with such a good runner, the hare lay down beside the woods to take a nap until the tortoise should catch up. Meanwhile, moving at a slow and steady pace, the tortoise soon passed the place where the hare was sleeping.

The hare slept on very peacefully until at last when he did wake up, the tortoise was almost at the finish line. Now the hare ran as fast as he could, but he was not able to overtake the tortoise in time, and the tortoise won the race.

The moral of the story is: "Slow and steady wins the race."

IN THE YEAR A.D. 50 the apostle Paul attended a very important church conference in Jerusalem. Immediately after this meeting of the leaders in the early Christian church, he set forth upon a missionary journey which took him into the central part of Asia Minor. The people who had settled in this area of the world were known as Galatians. They were people who had split off from the main migration of the Gauls who had moved westward through Macedonia and Greece into the country which we now call France. But like the Frenchmen of today, the Galatians in the time of Paul were an impulsive and highly unpredictable people. Consequently when Paul arrived with the Christian gospel, many men and women accepted Jesus Christ immediately, impulsively, and enthusiastically. To insure the permanency of his teaching in the hearts of these people, Paul stayed with them for some time, teaching and preaching the gospel from home to home, from day to day. When it was time for him to leave, Paul was sure that he had planted the gospel in good soil and that it would continue to grow and to take root again in the lives of others.

The days passed and Paul traveled on to carry the gospel into new and different lands. Then one day he heard that the Galatians, whom he once thought were firmly indoctrinated in the knowledge of Jesus Christ, were now turning their ears to the people known as Judaizers who were teaching a different gospel than that which Paul preached. The

Judaizers insisted upon the observance of the Jewish law in all things and to the very letter! The poor Galatians, who were once so exuberant over their freedom in the gospel, were now becoming servants of the law.

The apostle Paul, filled with a sense of righteous indignation, sat down to write a letter to his friends in Galatia. Without bothering to consider the usual compliments with which he started all of his other letters, Paul immediately launched forth into a discussion of the meaning of man's salvation by faith in Jesus Christ. He reminded the Galatians of his visit with them and the words which he taught them. He devoted a whole chapter in his letter to these fast-running hares—these people who started well in the faith and then seemed to get lost along the way. Then Paul asked a most startling question: "You were running well; who hindered you . . .?" (Gal 5:7, NASB).

Paul wanted to know what happened to those people who, one time not so long ago, so eagerly accepted the gospel of Jesus Christ, and who literally raced into the bosom of the Christian church. For a while they seemed to be advancing and running forward so well toward the prize of their high calling in Jesus Christ. Then suddenly something happened, and Paul, using the analogy of a race, said, "What did happen? Who stopped you? Or was it that, like the hare of old, you simply became tired and stopped in the shade of a tree to rest, never to resume the journey again?"

The question which Paul asked the Galatians is also the question which we must ask ourselves. We remember how we began the race in life. We remember the vigor and the confidence that we once had as children of faith. Now we must ask the question, What has happened? Have we become tired? Have we become overconfident in our own knowledge of the Word of God and the promise of His love?

Do we refuse the work and the labor and the offices of the church simply by saying that we have done well and that we are now going to rest for a while in the shade of a tree, not realizing that the race may well be over before we have a chance to become contenders again? Could it be that perhaps we have a reputation for being front-runners, and since our reputation has not been challenged for so long a period of time we are now unfit and unable to maintain the pace which once brought us into the forefront of the world's attention? Could the lack of a challenge have caused us to become careless and undisciplined to the point that we cannot now maintain the pace which we once easily set? Could it be that through the lack of any systematic form of training we have become short-winded and out of breath in the time of our present testing?

We started well in this life, but something has overcome us. Something has brought us down. In the course of time we have lost our ideals and we have buried our good intentions and our ambitions have become our frustrations. Now instead of searching for life anew, we seek to find a resting place in the shade by the side of the road.

This is exactly what happened to some of the people in the early church in Galatia. This is exactly why Paul was forced to write them such a strong letter beseeching them to rise up and to press forward toward the goal, the finish line, that prize of their high calling in Jesus Christ, our Lord. This is all that Paul could do for the Galatians. He could not run the race for them. He could not go back to that land which he left so many weeks ago to lift each person and carry him across the finish line. So Paul ends his letter to the Galatians with this word of advice: He urges every man to help every other man—to awaken and to restore those who have fallen into places of shady rest by the side of the road; he urges every man to bear the burdens of others—to prove and to test his own work, and at the same time to bear his own load in life. Thus Paul implores the Galatians to move forward by the power of the Spirit of God.

This is the challenge which Paul presents to us, that we should not be weary in this race of life, but that we should consider the life of Him who ran this course before us and for us. We should consider again the rule of life which He gave us and then remember that "Those who will walk by this rule, peace and mercy be upon them" (Gal 6:16, NASB). Thus may we discipline ourselves in the faith, may we once again be reminded to maintain a rigorous schedule of worship at home and in the sanctuary of the church. Being so disciplined and so trained we may continue to our life's end upon the course which He has marked for us. And our course is marked. Our way is set forth in the example of Him who lived for us and died for us. This is what Paul tells us again and again.

Run we must, and may the day never come when we shall hear those horrible words as we sit under the shade of a Judas tree, "You ran so well; what stopped you?"

HOIST WITH HIS OWN PETARD

Once upon a time a goat and a donkey were kept in the same barn by their owner. The goat became very jealous of the donkey because the donkey always had food enough and some to spare. So to taunt the donkey the goat said, "Your life is one of never ending work, what with turning the millstone all day and carrying heavy loads. Take my advice. Pretend to trip and fall down every once in awhile so that you can rest."

The donkey took the goat's advice but was seriously injured when he fell. The owner sent for the veterinarian and after looking at the donkey, he prescribed a broth made from goat's meat as a cure. So they killed the goat to heal the donkey.

The moral of the story is: "To lay a trap for someone else is often to become the author of your own ruin."

WHEN WE WERE YOUNG, my brother and I used to play a game as we walked to school. It was a simple game. The basic idea was to avoid stepping on the cracks in the sidewalk. But if through fault we did misstep and chance upon a crack, then we felt the immediate compulsion to step on another crack, in order that the count would be even. Everything had to be even.

Since that day my brother and I have learned, as you probably have already learned, that things in life do not always come out even. In fact, it is the unevenness of life that often makes it so very interesting. This is an important lesson that we all have to learn sooner or later, for getting even is one of life's greatest temptations. The desire for vengeance, for revenge, is one of the many pitfalls that precede human pratfalls. We are warned and admonished at this point by the apostle Paul that "Vengeance is mine; I will repay, saith the Lord" (Ro 12:19, KJV). This has been the stand of the church down through the ages, and restated by poets and authors in such climactic phrases as John Milton's allegation in *Paradise Lost*: "Revenge, at first though sweet, Bitter ere long back on itself recoils." Like the backlash of the whip, it cuts the hand that seeks it.

There is no better illustration of a man laying a trap to get even with someone else, only to become the author of his own ruin, than the account of Haman and Mordecai recorded in the book of Esther. Esther, you remember, was a young girl who was adopted by her cousin Mordecai and raised by him as his own. Esther, in faithful obedience, did everything that Mordecai commanded her.

It came to pass that Xerxes (called Ahasuerus in the biblical account), the king of the land, was seeking a wife to share the throne with him. All the young maidens of worth and beauty were brought before him so that he might take his choice of the fairest of them all. In this ancient form of our modern Miss Universe contest it was the girl Esther whom the king chose to be his bride.

Now Mordecai, Esther's benefactor, remained unknown to the king. One day as he sat at the gate of the city listening to the voice of the people, he overheard two of the king's servants as they conspired to kill the king. Mordecai hastened with this news to Esther and she in turn told the king. The two men were caught in the middle of their plotting and were convicted and hanged for their evil conspiracy.

In those days there was a young man named Haman in the palace, who was exceedingly ambitious for himself. One day the king promoted him to a position of authority above all the other princes. Haman became a chamberlain to the king and a prime minister to the people. Wherever he went, people bowed down in respect as he went by—all except Mordecai, the cousin of Esther. Haman saw that Mordecai did not bow down before him and became very angry. As the days passed, his irritation grew to the point that he became filled with fury every time he would see Mordecai, and he set his heart upon a way to get even with this insolent little Jew.

At last Haman went to the king with a plan that he had conceived in the darkness of the night, a plan of vengeance. He offered to pay ten thousand pieces of silver into the king's treasury if the king would permit him to destroy the Jews in the land, including Mordecai, who he said was not faithful to the king. Now Xerxes was not aware of the fact that Esther, his wife, was a Jewess nor did he know that she was raised by Mordecai. In his ignorance, the king consented to the plan of his prime minister. Haman, in the flush of early victory, sent news to all the districts and all the provinces that the Jews were to be destroyed.

When Mordecai received word of this new edict from

the king, he rent his clothes, put on sackcloth and ashes, and went forth into the streets in an apparent state of mourning. At last he went up into the king's palace. There he sent word to Esther, hoping that she might in some way intercede for him and for all her people.

Esther now put her plans into action. She went to the king and invited him to have dinner with her the next evening and asked that Haman his counselor should also eat with them. The king was delighted and looked forward to such an evening with Esther. When Haman was informed of the invitation, he was filled with joy to know that he found favor with the king and queen.

As Haman left the palace that night, thrilled with the prospect of tomorrow's glory, he saw Mordecai the Jew standing by the king's gate. Once again Mordecai refused to bow down before him. Haman was filled with anger so overpowering that he lost all sense of reason. He vowed then and there that he would get even with this little Jew. When he arrived home he instructed his servants to build a gallows fifty cubits high and in the morning he swore he would hang Mordecai from those gallows.

Now it so happened that on that night the king commanded that his servant read from the book of Chronicles, the history of the kings. In the course of his reading, the servant related the account of Mordecai the Jew and how Mordecai had once saved the king's life from the hands of those who sought to kill him. The king asked his servant what honor had been bestowed upon Mordecai for his action. The king's servant answered, "Nothing was ever done for him." Just at that moment Haman entered into the king's chambers. The king called out to him, saying, "Haman, what should I do for a man whom I would like to honor?" Haman, thinking that the king was planning a surprise for him, answered by reciting all the things that he would choose if he were being honored. When he was through the king said, "Depart now and make haste and do all these things which you have said unto Mordecai the Jew who sits at my gate." For a moment Haman could not believe his ears. He hated to think that he was going to have to do all these things for Mordecai the Jew.

There was still the evening to look forward to, so Haman returned to the palace to attend Queen Esther's banquet. He was always proud to be seen in the company of the king and the queen and he still hoped in his heart that maybe the king yet intended to honor him. But when they had finished eating, Queen Esther told the king of all the evil things that Haman had done. She told Xerxes how Haman was trying to destroy all the Jews in the land and that she in turn would be destroyed because she was a Jewess. Naturally when the king heard all these things his heart was filled with terror and disgust. In this moment of confusion he did not know what to do. Then one of his servants leaned over his shoulder and said, "The gallows which Haman has prepared are standing in his yard, fifty cubits high." Then the king said in a tone of final despair, "Hang Haman upon them." (See Est 7:9b-10.) And so they hanged Haman on the gallows which he had prepared for Mordecai.

So we have heard, and twice it has been said, "To lay a trap for someone else is often to become the author of your own ruin."

LOOK BEFORE YOU LEAP

Once upon a time a fox fell into a well, and although the well was not too deep, the fox was unable to get out again. After he had been in the well for what seemed to be a long time, a goat came by to get a drink. The goat thought that the fox had gone down into the well to drink and asked if the water was any good. "Why, it's the best in the whole country," said the sly fox. "Why don't you jump in and have some?"

The thirsty goat quickly jumped in and began to drink. Just as quickly the fox jumped on the back of the goat and from there leaped out of the well. The silly goat now realized what a predicament he was in. He begged the fox to help him out but the fox was already running off into the woods.

As he ran he turned back and said, "If you had half as much sense as you have beard, you would have thought about how to get out before you jumped in."

The moral of the story is: "Look before you leap."

ORDINARILY JESUS strikes us as being an attractive person
with the deep voice of a shepherd calling out to his sheep.
Ordinarily we see Him as a man who never wearies of de-
scribing the glories that await those who come after Him.
Ordinarily we see Jesus as one who offers security, peace,
and a new freedom in life.

Then all of a sudden we read these words in the New
Testament: "If anyone comes to Me, and does not hate his
own father and mother and wife and children and brothers
and sisters, yes, and even his own life, he cannot be My
disciple." Then to make the cost of discipleship perfectly
clear to all of us He added: "Which one of you, when he
wants to build a tower, does not first sit down and calculate
the cost, to see if he has enough to complete it? Otherwise,
when he has laid a foundation, and is not able to finish, all
who observe it begin to ridicule him, saying, 'This man began to build and was not able to finish'" (Lk 14:26, 28-30,
NASB).

It almost seems that instead of imploring men to follow
Him, Jesus repels men from Himself, warns men against
Himself. Instead of offering the many blessings of the gospel
He seems to be saying, "Count what it will cost you in this
life and see if you are equal to My demands of discipleship."
Instead of setting men's hearts on fire, He seems to be throwing cold water on them. Instead of encouraging men to give
up a former way of life, He seems to instill a certain fear in
our hearts that we might not be able to make the great leap
of faith. And Jesus seems to say, almost cautiously, "Look
before you leap."

Now if there is one phrase that has remained with us from
the writings of the existential philosophers, it would be that
phrase ascribed to Kierkegaard which he used to express the
idea of that movement which takes place in the heart of man

upon his acceptance of the gospel of Jesus Christ. This choice which man makes he calls the "leap of faith." Basically Kierkegaard states that every choice between the aesthetic, ethical, and religious type of life involves a leap. This leap, even though it is an inner, silent, and perhaps unobserved movement, implies a vast change in the life of an individual.

We stand upon this same brink of life, this chasm of faith. We are poised and coiled for this leap of faith. We are not unlike those people who were with Jesus upon His journey to Jerusalem. Jesus, who had so recently set forth from Nazareth to bring salvation to the world, was now approaching the city of Jerusalem, followed by the multitudes who seemed to gather around Him wherever He went. They hung on to His every word; they were impressed by His manner; for once, a new ray of hope gleamed from their eyes. The world seemed almost ready to snap the latch which would catapult Jesus forth as the Saviour of mankind, and many who followed after Him were now ready to make the leap of faith.

It was at this point, when all conditions of acceptance seemed favorable, that Jesus hesitated, looked at the eager and expectant faces of those who followed Him, and spoke to the crowd on the demands of discipleship. Now any professor of homiletics could tell you that this was not the best time for such a discourse. Any salesman will tell you that when your customer is ready to sign the purchase order you do not pause to remind him of the monthly payments! But Jesus did. He warned His followers of the conditions which they would have to accept. Then, still wondering if they understood the demands which would soon be made of them, He spoke this parable: "Which one of you when he wants to build a tower, does not first sit down and calculate the cost to see if he has enough to complete it?" Now this was a saying that the people could well understand. Who has not seen some task half completed and then abandoned because someone did not first sit down and count the cost?

Still we wonder why Jesus was so cautious at this time and so insistent that men should sit down and consider His demands and seriously look before they leap. We do not seem to be quite that concerned when people express their desire to unite with the church. We are formal and we do things decently and in order, but we are not overly demanding in our rules of discipline.

First, let us understand that Jesus was not afraid that men would fail Him, nor was He trying to make men fearful of failure. Not at all. These were not words of caution as much as they were words of common sense. Jesus demands that men make a choice. He demands that men make a leap, but He wants this leap to be due to an intelligent choice made with common sense and with good reason. He does not want us to jump blindly into the well. He does not want us to refuse to think, and therefore refuse to leap, any more than He wants us to leap without thinking.

Furthermore, Jesus is here warning us against the danger of living in a dream world. Jesus is asking us once again to face life realistically and to face ourselves honestly. No man today can, in good conscience, ever believe that the Christian life is a life which can be lived without a disciplined preparation day by day. If towers are going to be built in the world today, then people are going to have to plan for them, prepare for them, before they start to build them. If the life committed to Jesus Christ is going to be lived today, then people must plan for that life and prepare for that life realistically. We cannot leap into the pit of human existence blindly, under the false assumption that God will do for us what we have failed to do for ourselves. So look we must, if leap we will!

Perhaps now, in this context, we can understand the severe words of Jesus which preceded this parable, words which have all too often come to us as an offense to our sense of family loyalty and unity. Whoever "does not hate his own father and mother and wife and children and brothers and sisters, yes, and even his own life, he cannot be My disciple." We ask, How can this man Jesus, who demands that we love our enemies, at the same time require that we hate those who are closest and dearest to us? This contrast constrains us. We hesitate to accept it. But Jesus here is simply reminding us of a constant danger which we often overlook.

We casually think that it is only what we like to call the big immoralities of life, the big sins, that keep us from being perfect disciples. Jesus is trying to show us that the power of Satan is not limited to frontal attacks against our well-guarded sense of morality. In fact, Satan may very well attack our flank forces where we least expect him. He might even go so far as to use the love which we have for our children and families as a means of separating us from our devotion to God!

We hardly feel that such an occasion is possible, since God gave us our children and families, and since it is a natural and godly act to love them. It seems impossible that such a love could ever separate us from God. But the danger comes when we love our children to the point that they soon occupy the foremost place in our thoughts and affections when Jesus demands that primal place of importance Himself. Jesus was so emphatic in this demand that He said if a time comes when a choice must be made between loyalty to

Him and to those who are nearest and dearest to us, then we must choose Him.

Jesus knew something of the embarrassment of those who fail to look before they leap. He knew something of the embarrassment of those who started to build towers only to find out that they did not have enough money to complete the project once started. He also knows the frustrations which we will face in life if we attempt to be His disciples without considering the demands which will be placed upon us. It is to save us from this misery and despair that He demands that we sit down and consider the cost of discipleship, lest in moving too quickly in brash confidence we leave a trail of incompleted towers behind us, or lest in a euphoric sense of emotional enthusiasm we make the leap of faith without counting the cost and discover that we have landed in wells that are spiritually arid.

And now, be well reminded that Jesus Himself must have often considered the cost of discipleship. He alone knew the whole cost of our salvation. He alone knew the full weight of human sin. And He must have considered all these things when He said, "Not my will, but thine, be done!"

AN ASS IN A LION'S SKIN

Once upon a time a donkey found a lion's skin which had been left in the field by some hunters. The donkey put the skin on over his body and amused himself by roaming around in the woods frightening all the animals he met.

Then he went toward his own village. As he approached, all the inhabitants fled in fear. In his pride and delight he lifted up his voice and brayed. A fox who heard him came up to him and said, "Ah, my friend, I might have been frightened too if I had not heard your voice."

Then everyone recognized him and his owner came and gave him a sound beating for the scare he had caused.

The moral of the story is: "Outward appearances may disguise for a while, but words will disclose a fool."

MORE THAN ONCE in the course of history men have been trapped in their attempted disguises through the foolishness of their chattering. History records many instances where the spoken word determined the nature of a man's allegiance. In the small countries of Europe where the racial stock was so intermixed that it was impossible to distinguish the infiltraters from the indigenous population in time of war, the test of the spoken word was often used. For everywhere a man goes, his accentuation and pronunciation will reveal his true nationality. "In the Sicilian Vespers, March 31, 1282, the French were made to betray themselves by their pronunciation of 'ceci e ciceri'; those who pronounced the 'c' as in the French 'sessi et siseri' were hewn down upon the spot. When the revolt against the French in Flanders broke out, May 25, 1302, the gates were seized and no one was allowed to pass who could not utter the words—to a French tongue unpronounceable—'scilt ende friend?' "*

Even more than twenty-three hundred years before the revolt broke out against the French in Flanders, the test of accent was being put to use in Gilead by a man named Jeptha, a man who was raised up by God to deliver Israel in the hour of her need. However, he must have wondered in his early youth if God ever intended to use him or if God would ever choose him. He was the illegitimate child of a Gileadite who was expelled from his father's home through the demands of his brothers. He fled to the land of Harran where life was abundant and free for a man who was fleet of foot and skilled with a spear. In time and through his own ability as a huntsman and warrior, he was able to command a small band of roustabouts who chose him as their chief. However, even in this strange land, Jeptha was not a lawless renegade or a barbaric huntsman. On the contrary, he was a man with a conscience who feared God and sought in some way to serve Him.

*Phillips P. Elliott, "Judges," in *The Interpreter's Bible* (Nashville: Abingdon, 1953), 2:774.

Now at this same time the Ammonites had invaded the land of Israel and they were holding it in subjection. The elders in Gilead, those men who had driven Jeptha away, now needed this mighty warrior to deliver them from the hand of the Ammonites. So Jeptha returned and assumed the primary position of leadership. In true political fashion his first act was to invite the neighboring tribe of Ephraim to help in the battle of the Gileadites. But the Ephraimites were deaf to his pleas. So alone, Jeptha and his small army went forth to wage war against the Ammonites.

Now from the very beginning of his ten years as ruler over the people of Gilead, Jeptha knew that the issue of war was in the hands of God. And it was by the grace of God that Jeptha did defeat the Ammonites.

The Ephraimites had seen the success of the Gileadites in their victory over the Ammonites and they became jealous in their desire for the spoils of war. Immediately they became extremely critical of the great commander who won this victory without their help. They complained about Jeptha and called his men fugitives, renegades, men without a country, opportunists. So the Ephraimites, in their irrational frenzy, were easily led to cross the Jordan and seek release from their own frustrations by waging war against Jeptha. Jeptha in turn gathered all the men of Gilead and met the men of Ephraim in battle.

It is recorded that the Gileadites smote the Ephraimites that day, and even went down to the passes of the Jordan River to cut off the retreat of the Ephraimites who had escaped from the battle. There the men of Gilead stopped all the fleeing Ephraimites. When those from Ephraim sought to go across the river to escape again into their homeland, the men of Gilead, being unable to recognize them through any racial differentiations said, "Art thou an Ephraimite?"

and if the men from Ephraim said no, then the men from Gilead would say to them, "Say now [the word] Shibboleth," and the Ephraimites would answer "Sibboleth" for they could not pronounce it right. Then the men of Gilead took the escaping Ephraimites and slew them at the passages of the Jordan and the water ran red with the blood of forty-two thousand of the sons of Ephraim. (See Judg 12:1-9.)

The years passed and once again in the course of history we see where a man's voice betrays him. A simple test to be sure, but even a man as great as the apostle Peter was trapped by it. On that darkest night of human history— when Jesus was betrayed by the kiss and seized and led away into the home of the high priest—Peter followed at a distance. When they had kindled a fire in the courtyard outside the home, Peter sat down with Christ's captors. A maid who saw him in the light of the fire gazed at him for a moment and said, "This man was with Him too." But Peter denied it and said "Woman, I do not know Him." A little while later someone else said, "You are one of them too!" and Peter said, "Man, I am not." Then after an interval of about another hour, someone else insisted and said, "Certainly this man also was with Him for he is a Galilean too" (see Lk 22:54-59, NASB). It was his Galilean accent which linked him so conclusively as a disciple of Christ.

So also our lives are constantly being tested. No matter what we try to appear to be to others, the accent of our life often gives us away. People can readily discern whether or not our lives are Christ-oriented no matter how we try to disguise our words and deeds. Even when we feel least threatened by public discovery, some casual slip of the tongue reveals our true character, or some careless action reveals our lack of Christian concern for others. It was in knowledge of this that Jesus said, "Not everyone who says to Me, 'Lord, Lord,' will enter the kingdom of heaven" (Mt 7:21, NASB). Once again we are reminded that outward appearances may disguise, but words will disclose a fool.

KILLED BY KINDNESS

Once upon a time a monkey gave birth to twins. It so happened that the mother monkey gave all of her love to one of the twins while she constantly corrected and criticized the other. One day the mother held the favorite monkey to her breast so tightly that he smothered and died. The twin that was rejected grew to maturity and lived a happy and useful life.

The moral of the story is: "A child can be killed by kindness."

WE ARE ALL FAMILIAR with the little girl "who had a little curl right in the middle of her forehead; and when she was good, she was very, very good, but when she was bad she was horrid!" Children today are still the same. They can be wonderful, they can be horrible. They can be enjoyable, they can be vexacious. Then can be orderly or disorderly, generous or greedy, spritely or sullen, considerate or cruel.

30

But no sooner do we say these things about children than we realize that we have noted these same pleasant and unpleasant behavior characteristics in our relationships with adults. However, to avoid incriminating the members of that mature society known as adulthood, let us examine the world of childhood experiences.

We may draw a primary conclusion which should lead us to understand that children live in a world of tension even as adults do. Children are faced with physical and psychological threats even as adults are. Consequently when their little world is threatened, they too become tense and anxious, suspicious and fearful, and even hostile, just like their parents. After all, they are human!

This is by no means an attempt to condone or excuse their unsocial or uncivil behavior, but neither does it mean that we should preclude any attempt to understand that children often behave the way they do, not because they choose to, but because (like their parents) it is the only way they know to defend themselves from some of the threats of human existence. Thus the task of adults becomes that of helping children find socially acceptable ways of dealing with these life-threatening situations, these traumas and tensions, just as we are constantly learning socially acceptable ways of handling our own problems.

But how? What can we say to Mrs. Jones whose children Johnny, Jimmy, and Janie are known throughout the neighborhood and surrounding areas as three holy terrors? They have been known to hit, to bite, to scratch—not only each other, but any other child who is brave enough to venture forth to play with them. They are like a tornado outside the home. They are like a cyclone within the home. They act like animals at the table and their manners when company is present represent those of some savage tribe long since extinct from the face of the earth. Their poor mother is on the verge of a total nervous breakdown, and in exasperation she cries out for help, in every direction. And from every direction she hears experts answering her plea saying, "Give them love!" But she counters, "That is just what I have been giving them ever since the day they were born!" In the true sense of biblical love she has never been overly harsh or unkind to them. She has always been considerate, calm, patient, and tolerant of their faults. Now in final desperation she cries out again, saying, "Tell me what's wrong."

In simple language, a part of the answer may be that love is not always enough. Love is often only half of the prescription of keeping children well-adjusted and secure. The other half of this prescription is discipline. So said Solomon, "He that spareth his rod hateth his son" (Pr 13:24, KJV). Aesop also reminds us that children can truly be killed by kindness!

It is unfortunate that the word *discipline* has fallen into disrepute since the days of Aesop and Solomon. We think of discipline today as being some sort of stern punitive treatment which is meted out in painful measures. Those familiar with the military way of life associate discipline with their recruit training days or their basic training. Etymologically, the word *discipline* comes from *disciple*. The word *disciple* refers to one who follows the teachings of his master or leader. Discipline is a form of inspiration and guidance by precept and example to help children regulate their behavior as they grow up. At times discipline may mean saying "No" or "You must not." At times discipline may mean that you will have to scold your child if an order is disobeyed. It may even mean having to punish the child to cause him to stop a continued form of disobedience. But above all, even in its sternest form, discipline should always be used only to teach a child to control his behavior, and never as an example of a parent's lack of control over his own behavior.

The obvious question now becomes, How much discipline should we use with our children, and what kind of discipline ought we to administer? Knowing that this problem has been argued for centuries by the greatest minds of the world, we would not presume to propose to settle the issue here. However, in the Christian home we should avail ourselves of the biblical suggestions which guide us in giving our children the type of discipline which will reduce their tensions and problems as well as our own. First of all we must understand that, as with all problems, the problem of discipline also presents two extremes, one on either side of the middle path. We will do well to give equal consideration to both extremes before we examine the middle path.

On the one extreme there are parents who feel that children should grow in freedom of expression without the rigid restraints of domineering discipline. These parents feel that it is harmful to inhibit children because it might give them complexes which will plague them in later life. Unfortunately they let their children have their own free way in everything. The minor tragedy is that these parents have based their thinking on the words of the apostle Paul when he admonished the Colossians saying, "Fathers, provoke not your children to anger, lest they be discouraged" (Col 3:21, KJV). This admonition is often interpreted as "Fathers, do not overdiscipline your children." Consequently many parents today are afraid of correcting their children for fear of overdisciplining them and frustrating them.

On the other extreme there are parents who believe that children are naturally prone to do that which is evil and consequently they should be watched and corrected at every step of the way. These people are not so much parents as they are policemen who make their helpless children feel like criminals, constantly under the veil of suspicious surveillance. Unfortunately these parents also base their thinking on the words of the apostle Paul as they are recorded in his letter to the Ephesians: "Children, obey your parents in the Lord: for this is right" (Eph 6:1, KJV). The danger of this overemphasis on discipline is obvious in the lives of children who rebel whenever they feel they are not being watched.

Somewhere in between these two extremes lies the Christian approach. Children need a certain amount of discipline to teach them how to live safely and peacefully with others, but when discipline goes beyond that point it becomes a burden which is unbearable for a child, producing nothing more than resistance and negative results. Even as children cannot have complete freedom in life, neither can parents continually retain a vise-like grip upon them.

To sum it all up, somewhere in the wisdom literature of old, somewhere in that preliterate advice of the sages, parents were solemnly instructed with these words, which first pertained only to clothing: "Wide will wear, but tight will tear!" A world of human experience is bound up in the simple phrase, not only relating to garments and clothing, but also relating to this problem of discipline in the home. To be sure, fairness is essential, but firmness is important! A child is more than a lump of human clay left on this earth to be molded by his parents. He is also an expression in himself of all the forces of nature. The fairness and the firmness of discipline lies in the parents' ability to help the child realize the full expression of his individuality within the bounds of moral propriety, that the child be neither killed by kindness nor destroyed by dominance!

THE TREES AND THE BRIAR
BUSH

Once upon a time all the trees in the forest decided to choose
a king from their midst. So they said to the olive tree, "Will
you be our king?" But the olive tree answered, "Do you expect
me to give up my richness, my oil which God and man admire
in me just to rule over the trees?"

So the committee of trees selecting a king said to the fig tree,
"Will you be our king?" And the fig tree said, "Do you expect
me to give up all my good fruit and sweetness just to be your
king?"

Then the committee said to the briar bush, "Will you be our
king?" And the briar bush, which had never before been popular in the forest, answered, "If you really want me to be your
king, come and stand in my shade. If you do not, then may fire
come from the briar to destroy you all."

The moral of the story is: "We get the rulers we deserve."

SINCE THE DEATH OF JOSHUA, the children of Israel had been delivered from the hands of their oppressors by a series of capable judges: Othniel, Ehud, Deborah, Shamgar, and Gideon. But then after the death of Gideon, the Israelites turned away from God. Without a leader to govern them, they turned once again to the worship of false gods. Gideon had seventy sons, none of whom seemed overly anxious to become judge over all Israel. Gideon also had one illegitimate son named Abimelech who was not only desirous of becoming the judge over all Israel, but who was also determined to hold that high office.

Abimelech was so determined that he went to the home of his mother's kinsman in the city of Shechem, and there he addressed the citizens and put a question to them. "Is it better for you that all the sons of Gideon, which are three score and ten persons, reign over you, or that one reigns over you?" In other words he said, "Would you like to have seventy kings or one king?"

Abimelech's question sounded logical, so the people of Shechem came together again and they pronounced Abimelech king. He was crowned under the large oak tree in the city of Shechem. (See Judg 9:1-6.)

When young Jotham heard the news of this coronation ceremony, he quickly went to the region of Shechem and came to the top of Mt. Gerazim, and then he lifted up his voice and spoke a fable to all the people who had assembled. He said,

> Hearken unto me, ye men of Shechem, that God may hearken unto you. The trees went forth on a time to anoint a king over them; and they said unto the olive tree, Reign thou over us. But the olive tree said unto them, Should I leave my fatness, wherewith by me they honour God and man, and go to be promoted over the trees? And

the trees said to the fig tree, Come thou, and reign over us. But the fig tree said unto them, Should I forsake my sweetness, and my good fruit, and go to be promoted over the trees? Then said the trees unto the vine, Come thou, and reign over us. And the vine said unto them, Should I leave my wine, which cheereth God and man, and go to be promoted over the trees? Then said all the trees unto the bramble, Come thou, and reign over us. And the bramble said unto the trees, If in truth ye anoint me king over you, then come and put your trust in my shadow: and if not, let fire come out of the bramble, and devour the cedars of Lebanon (Judg 9:7-15).

If ye then have dealt truly and sincerely with Jerubbaal and with his house this day, then rejoice ye in Abimelech, and let him also rejoice in you: But if not, let fire come out from Abimelech, and devour the men of Shechem, and the house of Millo; and let fire come out from the men of Shechem and the house of Millo, and devour Abimelech (Judg 9:19-20).

And after saying all of this, Jotham ran away and he went to Beer and lived there because he was now afraid of Abimelech his brother.

The moral of this fable is quite simple. The trees had chosen as their ruler a bramble bush who had offered them, in return for his office, the privilege of taking refuge in his shade. The bush that gives no shade has offered shade as a reward to its constituents! All the trees had heard the condition under which the bramblebush stated that it would be willing to serve; they heard it boast of a protection that it was unable to give; they heard it promise a service that it was not able to render, and yet these trees, in their desire to have a leader and in their desire not to be involved in the responsibility of leadership themselves, chose to take refuge in the shade of a bush that was unable to produce any shade.

We ask, Why would the trees elect a bush as their king?
To bring the fable into the proportions of our own experience we might ask, Why are so many inadequate men elected
to positions of high public office? Why are dishonest men
elected to positions of trust? Why are the weak elected to
lead the strong? Why are the incompetent elected to direct
the competent? Is this not so often the case in the life of the
church when an organization within the structural fellowship
of the congregation becomes weak and ineffective for lack of
leadership? Yet how many people have been asked to be
the president of a group for only one year—just one year—
and have, with a loud voice and a thousand excuses, refused?
But the group, the organization, in order to survive, must
have a leader and so someone—some willing soul (no matter how unqualified for the office he may be)—is elected.
Though he promises shade and comfort, he has neither the
ability nor the potentiality to produce that which he promises.

To be sure, the trees knew the worthlessness of the bramblebush; but they elected him nonetheless as their leader.
The organizations know the inefficiency and inaptness of
many of their members; yet they elect them to positions of
leadership and authority.

Let us then understand this fable, not as a condemnation
of the bramblebush, but as a condemnation of the trees that
elected the bramblebush as their king. Likewise, to extend
the moral of the story, Jotham is not criticizing Abimelech
as much as he is criticizing the citizens of the city of
Shechem. To carry the analogy a little further into our own
experience today, groups and organizations which complain
of the lack of leadership might find that the complaint rests
not on the leaders elected as much as upon those members

of the organization who, like the trees, were not desirous of bearing the brunt of responsibility themselves.

There are men today like the olive trees of old who are not at all desirous to leave the productive tasks of life to which they feel they have been called (due to a modicum of success) simply to go and lead other people to Christ and deal with their problems. There are also men like the fig tree of old who are not anxious in the least to leave the sweetness and the heady pleasures of this human life to become involved in the problems of civic and ecclesiastical responsibility. There are men like the vine of old who are not at all anxious to leave the pursuit of the fruit of the world in order to take up the fruitless pursuit of trying to resolve some of the mundane problems of modern community life. In brief, man is by nature not eager to be the servant of others and thus it is that a bramblebush can often become the king over the trees.

As citizens of the kingdom of God we need to be constantly reminded of our own responsibilities in accepting the call to Christ's service, which is the constant claim of the church upon our lives.

INCURABLE

Once upon a time there was a woman who thought of a plan to cure her husband from drinking. She waited until a time when he was dead drunk, and then, lifting him up upon her shoulders, she carted him off to the local cemetery and put him in a tomb. When she thought that he had had time enough to sober up, she went back and knocked at the door of the mausoleum.

"Who's there?" he called from inside, and she answered that she was bringing an offering for the dead.

When she heard no answer from within, she spoke again and said that she was bringing a gift of food. Then her husband cried out from inside the tomb, "Away with your food, woman! I don't want food. I want drink!"

Then the woman beat her breast and said, "Woe is me! Instead of teaching my husband a lesson, I've only made him worse. His weakness has become a habit."

The moral of the story is: "There will come a time when even if a person wants to, he cannot break his habits."

OCTOBER MARKS that time of the year when the swallows will leave their roosts and their nests in Capistrano and fly south for the winter. These little birds will wing their way south, traveling from three to five thousand miles as they fly toward sunnier and warmer climates. These fine-feathered flying machines, weighing only a few ounces, will find a place in the South to spend the winter. Then they will return again in the spring on that special day in March which marks the swallows' return to Capistrano.

But I wonder why. I can't understand why a swallow goes to all the bother of flying all the way south to find a comfortable land where insect food is readily available only to turn around again and fly that whole distance back simply to return to Capistrano! Why don't the swallows stay where they are? They have plenty of food. They have the climate they need for survival. What is it that would bring them back again to Capistrano?

Now, I am no ornithologist; in fact, I am not even a member of the Audubon society. Yet, to my way of thinking, it sometimes seems as though some birds migrate simply out of habit and not out of necessity, especially when swallows leave sunny southern California. I could understand their leaving the frozen tundra of the Northland (when I would well like to travel south myself), but it is hard for me to understand why the swallows would leave a warm climate for another warm climate. I have wondered perhaps if maybe this is but the result of an ancient habit which has continued long after its imperative need has been forgotten, a habit which goes back much further than we dare think.

From the time of Pliny the Elder in the first century A.D., who began to investigate the habits of migrating birds, until the present time, there have been innumerable views put forth as explanation of these habits. Today, some naturalists have become quite convinced that these migratory patterns can be simply described as habits and that the time has come when the swallows can well abandon such old habits. The time has come when they can deliver themselves now from the burden of traveling the thousands of miles they travel every year, and yet they continue.

So often in nature we find almost the mirror of man, almost the same picture of what we do ourselves. The habits which we well have the power to break, the habits that consume our time and our energy, the habits which waste our productivity, are the habits that still hold us in bondage; and sometimes we do not even know why.

We do things daily out of habit simply because methods and means have been handed down to us through the years, often without rhyme or reason. Having liked the habits of the ages so well, we repeat them to ourselves as habit forces us to move in wasted effort.

But think of the swallows of Capistrano. Not all the swallows will return. Some swallows will perish in the flight. Some swallows will not be able to travel due to incapacitations later acquired. Some will prefer the new environment which they will find. Not all the swallows will return to Capistrano. This, I feel, is the great pity in the whole of our existence. Not many of us will be able to return later to a way of life which we once chose when we first followed the Christ. For many will wander into habits which will debilitate them. Others will acquire habits of religious neglect which will be hard to overcome. Some will venture into a far country never to return to the faith of their fathers, the faith of their youthful ardor.

It is something of this nature that Jesus had in mind when He said, "Every one who commits sin is the slave of sin" (Jn 8:34*b*, NASB). Once we make the journey, like the swallows, away from the Capistrano of our faith, we become slaves to the habits that bind us and shackle us. Much as we would like to break the habits that hold us and free ourselves from the fetters that bind us, we become, in spite of ourselves, slaves to that sin. We try and try to overcome and overpower the habits we detest, but our efforts are in vain. The habits may be as old as the centuries or they may be of our choosing and devising as of this day, but their grip is equally strong. We know all too well how we are enslaved to the habits that bind us. We know full well how we have enslaved ourselves to some of the sinful habits which we have appropriated to ourselves. Though we would like to deliver ourselves from the bondage that holds us, we find that we are being gripped tighter and tighter and the words of Jesus ring true as true can be. "Every one who commits sin is the slave of sin." Once a man begins a habit, he becomes a slave to that habit.

In Lord Byron's poem "The Prisoner of Chillon," written in the year 1816 when he visited Switzerland, Byron relates the imprisonment of the Boonivard brothers in a dungeon cell where they were chained to a wall. He tells of the death of the two younger brothers, the shallow graves in which they were buried, the bird that flew into the dungeon cell and kept the elder brother company there for a spell, the thoughts he thought which were each day the same, until at last his freedom came:

> At last men came to set me free;
> I asked not why, and recked not where;
> It was at length the same to me,
> Fettered or fetterless to be . . .
> My very chains and I grew friends,

So much a long communion tends
To make us what we are.

This is the story of our habits. Though we would gladly
deliver ourselves from them, we have become enchained to
them—"So much a long communion tends to make us what
we are."

But even as I pity those few swallows who will never return to Capistrano, I would like, at the same time, to extend
a word of congratulations to those that do return. Even if
their flight was unnecessary, and to my way of thinking,
quite a waste, I would like to congratulate those swallows
that do return!

In the same light, I would like to congratulate another
who also returned home after a long and wasted journey into
a far country, the prodigal son. This lad, who went into a
far country and took with him his inheritance and wasted it,
at last came to his senses. He rose up and said, "I will go to
my father and I will say to him, 'I have sinned before thee
and God; now make me as one of thy servants.'" (See Lk
15:12-19.) So the son went home. This prodigal son who
has been criticized and castigated from pulpit and platform
for years and years is now, I think, due for a word of con-
gratulation. This young man, who has been accused of almost every sin known to mankind, at least had the ability
to come to his senses and break away from such actions
which in time would have so possessed him as habits that he
would have been forever fettered to them. For this alone he
deserves our congratulations!

Here was a son who returned. And if we would ever want
to try to summarize the doctrine of grace in the New Testament, it could be summed up in the last passage of Christ's
reference regarding those who are trapped in the habits of

sin. When Jesus said, "Every one who commits sin is the slave of sin," He also added, "[But] If the Son makes you free, you will be free indeed."

We have, like the animals of nature, bound ourselves to habits and actions which, if we look at them, are not only sinful but also meaningless and sometimes much to our own detriment. We would gladly break these habits, but we feel that we do not have the power. Thus Jesus says, "If the Son makes you free, you will be free indeed," and this is our freedom! Herein we can break the shackles that bind us; herein we can break the habits that would destroy us.

Our help is in Christ who has overcome sin and the power of sin. It is this help that God offers us. It is this power that He gives us through the work of the Holy Spirit that we may be free! Unlike the husband in Aesop's fable, we are not incurable. Let us thank God for this power which is ours through Jesus Christ, our Lord.

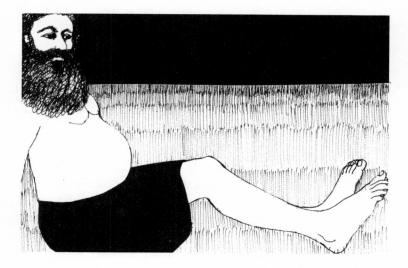

THE BELLY AND THE FEET

Once upon a time the belly and the feet were arguing about their individual merits and strength. The feet were saying to the belly that they certainly were stronger, for the feet actually had to carry the belly everywhere it went.

The belly answered, "That may be true, but if I stopped giving you nourishment you wouldn't be able to walk at all."

The moral of the story is: "To strike against a fellow member is to strike against yourself."

WHEN THE APOSTLE PAUL wrote to that small group of members who were united in one body known as the Christian church in Corinth, he was intent above all else to illustrate the need for a Christian ethic within the church. The understanding and application of that ethic become the core of the letter to this early Christian congregation. In the course of his epistle it became necessary for Paul to analyze and appraise the individual use of spiritual gifts. Paul emphasized that there were varieties of gifts within the church which were all given by the same Spirit of God. There were also varieties of service, but all under the direction of the same Lord. To each man, says this apostle, has been given the manifestation of the Spirit for the common good.

To make his point exceedingly clear, Paul used the analogy of the body, which also is one, but which has many members:

> For the body is not one member, but many. If the foot should say, "Because I am not a hand, I am not a part of the body," it is not for this reason any the less a part of the body. And if the ear should say, "Because I am not an eye, I am not a part of the body," it is not for this reason any the less a part of the body. If the whole body were an eye, where would the hearing be? If the whole were hearing, where would the sense of smell be? But now there are many members, but one body. And the eye cannot say to the hand, "I have no need of you"; or again the head to the feet, "I have no need of you." On the contrary, it is much truer that the members of the body which seem to be weaker are necessary; . . . And if one member suffers, all the members suffer with it; if one member is honored, all the members rejoice with it (1 Co 12:14-26, NASB).

In using this analogy, Paul realized that his audience would appreciate its authenticity as well as its humor. Livy, that famous Roman historian (59 B.C.—A.D. 17), tells us that in the year 494 B.C., when the Plebians seceded from Rome, a messenger from the city was able to calm the rebellion and convince the commoners to refrain from their folly of revolting by telling them an old "once upon a time" fable which was first attributed to Aesop, a Greek. So the revolting Plebians in their day heard the wise story of the feet who had a grievance against the belly because the belly never seemed to do any of the work but consumed all of the food. The feet went on strike and refused to work. But it wasn't long before they realized that they were simply striking against themselves. It was thus that the Plebians (the feet) realized that the Patricians (the belly) nourished the other members while they were in turn being nourished.

It was Paul's literary genius which brought this ancient fable, so recently used in a popular sense by the Romans, into the heart of his letter to the Corinthians. It was in this manner that Paul wanted to let these early churchmen know that God had granted to the church many gifts which differed in order and appropriateness. In this letter Paul mentioned eight gifts which the Spirit bestowed upon the church, eight gifts which emphasized the diversity of service within the church:

> God has appointed in the church, first apostles, second prophets, third teachers, then miracles, then gifts of healing, help, administrations, various kinds of tongues (1 Co 12:26-28, NASB).

Much of this same division of labor is evident in light of the church today. In Samuel Blizzard's *The Minister's Dilemma,* the work of the church is aptly divided into two major categories: the traditional role of the teacher, preacher, and priest; and the contemporary role of the functioning organizer and administrator. All too often the life of the church becomes involved in a grinding clash between these two major factions. At last men almost come to wonder whether life in the Spirit is under the care of shepherds or under the lash of sheep drivers! We wonder if the primary function of the church is to bear Christ to the people as did Mary of old, that He might be literally born into the world; or whether Christ, who has been born in Bethlehem, should now be administered in an organized and systematic manner to the masses who seek to be a part of His body. Like the fable of old, we have now entered again upon that debate. Once again we find the belly (a traditional role of the church) arguing with the feet (a contemporary role of the church) about their special services and virtues 'which give the necessary strength to the whole body of the church.

Those who wish to reinforce the primacy of the traditional role of the church make great note of the fact that Paul has listed as the primary and secondary gifts those of prophecy and teaching. They note with unmasked joy that he has placed those tasks of church administration at the very bottom of his list. On the other hand, those who prize the contemporary role of the church are continually tempted to exalt the administrative aspects of the life of the church as being of primary importance in sustaining the body of Christ. Our contemporaries remind us that all the good intentions of the traditionalists would be of no value whatsoever if they were not programmed into the world by the organized feet of this administrative part of the body!

In truth, every man should aim at doing a certain amount of legwork or footwork within the life of the church. To be sure, organization has its place. But it also has its obvious limitations. It can come to the point that the church becomes so overorganized that it becomes disorganized! There comes a time when the machinery of organization and specialization simply cannot do the work of the individual. The end result is that often the larger the congregation, the less personal responsibility the individual feels for the legwork necessary in proclaiming the gospel. The emphasis is more and more shifted upon the paid employees of the church, who in turn tend to emphasize promotional values over the personal values of the gospel, until at last the human personality is perforated with IBM punch-card holes and Christ's labor of love becomes love's labor lost.

It was something of this nature that the children of Israel witnessed in their wanderings through the wilderness. It didn't take an engineering genius to realize that the tabernacle which they would transport through the desolate places would be no simple thing to carry. The curtains and the coverings, the altar and the candlesticks, to say nothing of the tent itself, would weigh no small amount. It becomes heartening then to read in the book of Numbers that the princes of Israel were also aware of the organizational and administrative problems of the tabernacle. Knowing a bit of the complexities of worldly affairs, they gave Moses a gracious gift of six wagons drawn by twelve oxen. This rightly ought to solve his transportation problems. Moses, who once learned from his father-in-law the need for delegating authority, turned over the transportation details of this problem to the sons of Levi. Now Levi's sons were divided into three clans: the sons of Gershon, the sons of Merari, and the sons of Kohath. It would be easy for any child to quickly tell you that the best way to divide these six wagons among the three tribes would be to give two wagons to each tribe. But Moses, unfamiliar as he was with our modern methods of streamlined church management, gave two wagons to the sons of Gershon and four wagons to the sons of Merari. To the sons of Kohath he gave none at all. Our first glance at this division of labor might lead us to say that the hands and the feet (Gershon and Merari) might rightly have some bitter feelings toward the belly (the sons of Kohath). If the three tribes are involved in the labor of transportation and only two are assigned wagons, it might at first seem that the other tribe would not be carrying its fair share of the load. Once again in biblical history we see the lesson of the belly and the feet being clearly acted out in a human situation.

But this lesson is not complete. Moses shows us here that there are some tasks in the life of the church that cannot be accomplished by the turning of wheels, not even big wagon wheels! There are some burdens in the church which are too precious to be committed to carts which are drawn by oxen and which simply have to be borne by hand. It was for this reason that Moses gave no wagons to the sons of Kohath, for they were entrusted with the transporting of the sacred vessels of the temple. These were objects so sacred that no wheel was allowed to carry them, and it was instead the privileged duty of the sons of Kohath to bear this burden upon their shoulders. Thus, even in the Old Testament, we see that the various members of the body (church) need one another.

Likewise in the New Testament, Paul gives us very clearly the illustration of the body of Christ, the church, which consists not of one member, but of many—all with different gifts. One member cannot say to another, "I have no need of you."

In his epistle to the Galatians Paul summarized this analogy of the body and its members. He exhorts those early Christians to "Bear ye one another's burdens, and so fulfill the law of Christ" (Gal 6:2, KJV).

In the church today we cannot say that as members we have no need of one another. Instead we ought to be aware of the fact that we are in constant need of one another, for this is the fellowship that is ours in the body of Christ in whom we are individual members.

Though we may have differing gifts, though the labors of some may seem to them almost unnoticed while others seem to have been overly noticed, though some may appear to be doing all the work while others seem content to do no work at all, we are reminded again through this ancient fable that in Christ we are completely and continually dependent upon one another.

THE STRONG AND THE WEAK

Once upon a time a horse and a donkey were taken on the same trip by their master. The donkey, who carried all the supplies, said to the horse, "If you would take a share of my load, it would save my life." But the horse refused to help, and it was not long before the donkey was worn out with fatigue and fell down and died. Then the owner took all the supplies off the dead donkey's back and put them on the horse's back, plus the hide of the donkey.

Then the horse began to complain, saying, "Look at me now. I wouldn't take the light load when I had a chance and now I have to carry everything—including the donkey."

The moral of the story is: "The strong should help the weak so that the lives of both might be preserved."

IT IS A PITY that Aesop was not alive in the days of Saul so that he might have given that same good advice to Abner,

Saul's cousin, the commander in chief of the army. As time passed, Saul and David, through jealousy, began to fight against each other. It was then that Abner began "making himself strong" in the house of Saul. Abner was an opportunist whose only concern was for himself. He was willing to use any occasion for his own advancement and reward. His philosophy was one of self-seeking and self-fulfillment. But one day this mighty warrior, who played upon the weaknesses of others, was confronted by a man of equal strength who stabbed him in the back under the fifth rib, and thus Abner died the death of a fool. Abner had never learned that the punishment of selfishness and self-seeking is one's own self-destruction and that the strong should help the weak so that the lives of all would be preserved.

In the New Testament, the apostle Paul was well aware of this wisdom of the ages, and he used this exhortation as a means of concluding his letter to the early church in Rome, saying, "We who are strong ought to bear the weaknesses of those without strength, and not just please ourselves" (Ro 15:1, NASB). The words of the text assure us that Paul associated himself with those who are strong; but before we place ourselves in the company of the apostle we must in some degree of honesty evaluate our present situation.

I am not altogether convinced that there are two kinds of men, the strong and the weak. My experience has led me to believe that we are all much more alike than we think. What divides us into the two camps known as the strong and the weak might simply be the outward means whereby we try to disguise our inner weaknesses. Our outward reactions may lead some people to believe that we are something other than that which we are, but we know that in truth we are all weak and wretched and bound by the sinfulness of our human desires and passions.

But what does Paul mean when he says that the strong are to help the weak? Who are the strong? It is not my intent to confuse the issue, but let us for the sake of the analogy move from the spiritual life to the natural life. Here we can presume that the strong are those who are up and about in good health moving from activity to activity. The weak, we would suppose, are those who are bedridden in homes, hospitals, and institutions throughout the country. By such standards I would consider myself exceedingly strong, for I have never been hospitalized, nor have I even felt the discomfort of a sickbed for any period of time. But in all honesty, in this point where my strength should lie, I must confess that I am exceedingly weak, for I am not able to bear or understand the infirmities of those who are sick in body. Therefore at this point of my weakness I must constantly ask for the grace and power of God to be able to minister to the needs of those whom the world would call weak.

To me it has often been the beauty of Christ's ministry on earth that He constantly stretched forth His hand to the weak, the sick, and the suffering. In their weakness and distress they had the strength of faith to be healed and to become His servants and disciples. Conversely, it is interesting to note that those who thought they were strong were in the final analysis quite weak, for in their confrontation with the living Christ they were unable to free themselves from the human passions which bound them. Thus in contrast to the strength of a leper we see the weakness of a rich young ruler. The strength of a blind man who regained his sight is seen in contrast to the weakness of a Roman centurion who could not see beyond his own self-interest. The strength of a poor sinner ashamed of his own failings must be seen in contrast to a Pharisee whose great strength and pride kept him from seeing his own faults.

Yes, the strong are not as strong as they think they are. Perhaps those who confess their own feelings of insecurity and who see themselves as sinners in the eyes of God have a strength that those who feel themselves to be strong do not possess.

The fact is that the strong all too often repress everything that betrays their weakness. Frequently the disgust that they have for the weak rises from their own knowledge of their individual weaknesses. But in order to remain strong they find it necessary to overlook and override every weakness which is common to man.

Thus in what they consider to be strength, they refuse to admit that in certain aspects they too are weak. Those who prefer to dispense all things through their own power and are hesitant to admit that they need something, even to the point of being so careful not to show any signs of weakness, may refuse to admit that their lives are dependent upon the love of others. Unfortunately, at times they even resent the intimate love of family and the affection of close friends. In trying to maintain this facade of strength they become intolerable in their actions to the failings of those whom they consider to be weak, and the pity of it all is that they do not know that their attempt to be strong is their very sign of weakness.

Thus we who are strong ought to bear with the failings of the weak, lest all of us think that we are the strong who must tolerate the actions of others. Let us instead first be aware of our own failings and our own weaknesses. Let us first admit that we are all weak and all should be aware of our dependence upon others. Let us discover that we no longer need to use the bluster of false strength to cover up our own weaknesses.

If we understand this fact of our weakness, what then might be expected of us? The apostle Paul makes this point exceedingly clear—in our strength in Christ we are not to please ourselves, but "let each please his neighbor for his good." Our concern must be for our neighbor's success, for our neighbor's happiness. It is at this point that true strength becomes an observable fact. The man who is truly strong is that man who is not concerned about showing himself to be strong through some physical or material success, but who seeks instead to please his neighbor for his neighbor's good. It may sound silly that those who are strong in Christ are those who are not seeking this world's selfish means of using their strength and that the weak in truth are those who try so hard in this mortal life to appear strong. But to put this text into its simplest terms, let me remind you of a horse which, in great pride of its strength and power, laughed at a donkey that needed its help. Then with the apostle Paul, I would remind you that our task is not to congratulate ourselves upon our strength in Christ, but instead let each of us acknowledge our own weakness and learn to please our neighbors for their own good.

SHADOW AND SUBSTANCE

Once upon a time a dog was crossing a bridge over a small river and carrying a piece of meat in his mouth. Seeing his own reflection in the water, he thought that he saw another dog with a bigger piece of meat. In an attempt to snatch the bigger piece of meat away from the other dog, he opened his mouth and dropped out the piece of meat that he already had.

The result was that he had nothing. He could not get the other piece of meat because it didn't exist, and his own piece of meat which fell out of his mouth was swept down the stream by the swift current.

The moral of the story is: "People who always want more than what they have may end up with nothing at all."

TWO HUNDRED YEARS before Aesop related his fables there was a man named Naaman, who was a commander of the armies of the king of Syria. He was a great and mighty man of valor who was, unfortunately, afflicted with the loathsome disease of leprosy. But in God's good providence, Naaman was sent to Elisha the prophet to be healed. When Naaman washed himself in the river Jordan, according to the command of Elisha, his flesh was restored and he was clean! In his desire to thank God, Naaman offered a gift through Elisha in thanksgiving. But Elisha refused the generosity of the Syrian and sent him back to his own country. Gehazi, Elisha's servant, saw the shadow of prosperity and wealth over his own head. He was unable to resist the temptation to spring forth and run after Naaman's chariot until he stopped the Syrian commander, saying, "My master has sent me to say, 'pray give this man a talent of silver and two festal garments.' " Gehazi, his eyes bulging with greed, soon received that substance of material wealth which he so greatly desired. Soon Elisha discovered the duplicity of Gehazi's actions. All that Gehazi had, he lost; and to him was given instead the dreaded leprosy which once afflicted Naaman, and which now cleaved to Gehazi and his descendants forever. Gehazi, blinded by the shadow of that which he so desperately wanted, discovered that in reaching out for the substance he lost all that he had. (See 2 Ki 5:19-27.)

Years later, Jesus, in returning to His own hometown of Nazareth, was reminded of this Old Testament account. In coming home again, Jesus walked down the hills of Galilee across paths which He had known as a boy. In the distance He could see the village of Shunem where Elisha had lived and Mount Carmel where Elisha had walked.

Then Jesus entered into Nazareth and, as was His habit on the Sabbath, He went into the synagogue. There He read the lesson of the day from the prophet Isaiah, the sixty-first chapter, the proclamation of good news that was coming to the whole world. Then Jesus folded up the scroll, gave it back to the synagogue officer, and said, "Today this scripture has been fulfilled in your hearing" (Lk 4:21, NASB). The people who heard Him in His own synagogue were amazed and disturbed at the words which proceeded from His mouth, for they all knew Him as the young carpenter, the son of Joseph. Yet most recently they had heard of what had happened in Capernaum, and in His own life they had seen in His youth foreshadowings of what was to come. Jesus, realizing their thoughts, said, "You are bound to say to Me, 'Physician, heal thyself. We have heard what has happened in Capernaum; now do the same kind of things in this Your own country!' " To phrase it in colloquial terms, they said, "We have seen the shadows of Your greatness, but now let us see the substance! We have seen the graphic and descriptive reports of Your great works, but now let us see some actual miracles right here!" And the people waited for Him to perform a miracle. But Jesus said, "No prophet is accepted in his own country." Then thinking back through time Jesus added, "There were many lepers in Israel in the times of Elisha the prophet and none of them was healed—none but Naaman the Syrian." (See Lk 4:23-27.)

What really galled the members of that small congregation was that they who felt they owned God now had to listen to a man who told them that they had no special claim on God. These people who felt they were living in the very shadow of the Almighty were now being told that they did not really understand the substance of God's love. Furthermore, the substance of His being would now be carried by the stream of His love into the whole inhabited world. These people had not only lost the meaning of what Christ was trying to say to them, but in their desire for a greater hold on God they lost the grasp on that which they once possessed. It is no secret that today the congregation which wants to keep its churchly privileges to itself soon loses the vitality of its own existence. The church that is concerned only with its own business and seeks only to nurture its own life soon will be out of business and without life. Thus, in reaching for peripheral shadows, they are in danger of losing the basic substance of their existence.

This is exactly what happened to that congregation in Nazareth. In the mystery of human freedom they rejected the substance of Christ for the shadows of their religious doctrines. And in their own unbelief they hurt not only their own members, but they also hurt the larger parish— their neighbors who might have been healed by some miracle on the part of Christ.

These Nazarites were not far different from many people today who still demand of Jesus that He perform some kind of miracle in their lives that they might believe in Him. What an odd contortion of faith still exists, that men still demand to see the shadow of miracles before they put their trust in the substance of Christ! Those who were the close followers and true disciples were not those who were drawn to Him by their observations of His mighty works and miracles. Though His wonderful works drew crowds from near and far, His true disciples were those who obeyed His call and were influenced by His personal presence, the substance of His being (what Paul Tillich calls the "ground of all being"). It was in this substantial presence that their souls grew and grew as they too were admitted into the secret place of His spiritual life.

So the Christian church, the body of Jesus Christ, came into existence. But even in its earliest days it continued to wage war against the shadows of diversity and asceticism that sought to distract from the substance of Christ Himself. The apostle Paul, in a constant attempt to reveal the real truth of Jesus Christ, wrote in most of his letters—but particularly to the Colossians—something about the need to be able to differentiate between that which was essential to the faith, the very substance of Christ Himself, and that which was superficial, the shadow of faith. One of the most difficult battles which Paul had to wage was against the Colossian cultists who made strict observance of the external rules of religion—the shadows of superficial ritual—a substitute for the true substance of spiritual morality in Christ. Paul, who knew something about the tyranny of Pharisaic legalism and Jewish ritualism, was doubly emphatic in warning the Colossians about falling into the trap of reaching out for the shadow of religiosity and losing the very meaning of the substance of faith which is in Jesus Christ. Therefore he wrote to the Colossians, "Let no one act as your judge in regard to food or drink or in respect to a festival or a new moon or a Sabbath day—things which are a mere shadow of what is to come; but the substance belongs to Christ" (Col 2:16-17, NASB). Let no man fool you. Let no one deceive you. Let no people beguile you. For religion is not founded on eating and drinking or an abstinence from them, nor is it founded on the Jewish laws of festival observance. These things are only foretastes, shadows of real religion. The substance of real religion is fellowship with Christ. This is the substance of faith, that we should be in Christ.

To be concerned overly about eating, drinking, feasting, fasting, or the meticulous observance of all the rules and regulations of an ascetic abstainer leads a man not into Christ but into the sin of pride wherein he thinks he has found a way in himself to God without Christ. Such action is no more than slavery to the law, and not the intended freedom of faith. It was for this freedom that Christ set us at liberty. Such legalism led the Israelites into the shadow of the Almighty, but it was never meant to be the substance of their faith.

There are many today who are searching for the living substance of faith. There are many who are searching for the real Christ, for they know that He has the secret of this life and that knowing Him is to have life eternal. Heretofore they had only seen hazy reflections of this man Jesus and they had turned away without any spiritual nourishment from His substance. As pilgrims today let us continue to walk this spiritual road that we may help others to encounter the real Christ of the gospel narrative, and that we in our lives may never be found guilty of living in the shadows and losing the substance.

EXAMPLE IS BETTER THAN PRECEPT

Once upon a time there was a mother crab teaching her son how to walk. She admonished him not to walk sideways rubbing his sides against the wet rocks.

The son replied, "All right, Mother. If you want to teach me, first walk straight yourself. I'll watch you and follow your example."

The moral of the story is: "People who find fault with others ought to live straight and walk straight themselves before they attempt to instruct others."

LT. RALPH C. BETTERS, CHC, USNR, recently received the Navy Commendation Medal while serving in Vietnam. His citation read in part as follows: "At his own request he accompanied leading elements on search and destroy operations against insurgent Communist (Viet Cong) forces in Operation Starlight. Disregarding his own safety, he calmly joined the Marines in positions exposed to hostile fire, and by his own composure instilled confidence sorely needed by the younger men in their indoctrination into combat." It is this example of an officer, set for the benefit of those who followed him, which merited the receiving of the Navy Commendation Medal.

The example set by good and great men who are offering their lives for their country will never be forgotten, and their deeds will continue to live and to speak to all generations that succeed them. Their examples will live now in thought, in word, and in deed to guide us and to influence and direct us. The nobility of their character will pass into the hearts and the minds of those who follow after them as sources of inspiration and consolation in life and in death.

Even though medals are not always to be won in our everyday existence, we are reminded by the apostle Paul that we are to continually set an example to the rest of the world so that they might see our lives and glorify our Father who is in heaven. Paul was not in the least ashamed to admit that Christians are to be leaders in the world, instilling confidence and courage into those who are younger in the faith as they are indoctrinated into the trials of human existence.

Therefore, it was not vanity that prompted Paul to say to the members of that church in Philippi, "Brethren, join in following my example, and observe those who walk according to the pattern you have in us" (Phil 3:17, NASB). Paul was not referring to any righteousness on his part; he was referring to the need for all men to be imitators of Jesus Christ. Paul was in effect saying, "Imitate me in imitating Christ. We who are attempting to imitate Jesus Christ in our lives must also live such lives that others who may in turn be watching us might learn something of the love of God."

Paul also wrote to the Thessalonians reminding them of his bringing the gospel to them, saying, "You also became imitators of us and of the Lord . . . so that you became an example to all the believers in Macedonia and in Achaia" (1 Th 1:6-7, NASB). Paul knew something of the cultural barrier that had to be overcome in Thessalonica, and he knew that in imitating Jesus Christ the members of that early church would have to live lives which would be in total variance with the established cultural norms. Yet by so doing they also became examples to all those in Macedonia and Achaia. Moreover, Paul knew that no matter how eloquently he preached or how brilliantly he taught the gospel message, the final proof of its acceptance would be in the lives of those early believers. No wonder Paul rejoiced when the Thessalonians became examples to all people and their faith in God became known everywhere as testimony to the redemptive power of the incarnate Christ.

Likewise, when Paul's own authenticity as an apostle was being questioned by the church at Corinth, he answered the request for references not with letters of recommendation, but by reminding the members of that community that they themselves were his letters of recommendation (2 Co 3:2). Paul needed no testimonial other than the fact that the members of that early church in Corinth had followed his example in imitating Christ. Their lives then became his apostolic authority. They stood as greater proof of his apostleship than any written letter from the hand of man. The example set by the Corinthians in their daily lives as Christians was far more effective and fruitful than any written precept recorded by the judicatories of the early church!

Finally, by the time Paul wrote his letter to Timothy, a young minister in the church, it was no surprise that he stressed the great importance of the example which Timothy was expected to set among the lives of his parishioners. Paul, in his fatherly concern for Timothy and his continuing concern for the propagation of the gospel, wrote to this young pastor, "Be thou an example [to] the believers in word, in conversation, in charity, in spirit, in faith, in purity" (1 Ti 4:12). Timothy had to learn, as we all have to learn, that more people in this world will be influenced by what we do than by what we say. To a young pastor like Timothy it comes as a grave warning to learn to practice what you preach. I am always reminded of the severity of this warning to clergymen when my brother, who is a practicing physician, jokingly tells his friends that he practices whereas I simply preach! But Paul is insistent in reminding Timothy that if the gospel is to bear any fruit it will be through the example that we set with our lives, not simply by the words which we use. Chaucer, in his prologue to *The Canterbury Tales,* aptly phrases it:

> For if the priest be foul in whom we trust
> What wonder if a layman yield to lust?
> Well ought a priest example good to give,
> By his own cleanness, how his flock should live!

The apostle Peter, writing in the New Testament, is extremely conscious of the need of living as examples of the love of God. He reminds his readers, "For even hereunto were ye called: because Christ also suffered for us, leaving us an example, that ye should follow in his steps" (1 Pe 2:21, KJV). However, in his polished use of the language of the day, Peter uses a different word for "example" than did the apostle Paul. The word which Peter uses means "a child's writing copy." Those who still remember the Palmer method, whereby we learned to write by copying lines and circles over and over again, will be familiar with Peter's use of the word *example* which means a writing copy. Christ left for us, said Peter, an example which we could copy again and again until in constant repetition it becomes a way of life. Christ left no vague or abstract rules of human conduct, but a very specific and traceable plan for human existence. He left something that was readily visible which could be copied as easily as we copied the letters of the alphabet in our early educational training experiences.

This we confess is true; Christ has given us an example, and it is an example which we can understand and follow. Whenever we draw near to the holy table for the communion service we are again reminded of the example which Christ Jesus gave to His disciples. During the last supper, Jesus rose from the table and laid aside His garments and girded Himself with a towel. Then He poured water into a basin and began to wash the feet of His disciples. He wiped them with a towel. Even after their protestations He continued. When He was through, He put on His garments and resumed His place again, and said, "Do you know what I have done unto you? You call me Teacher, and Lord; and you are right; for so I am. If then the Lord and the Teacher washed your feet, you also ought to wash one another's feet, for I gave you an example that you should do as I did to you" (Jn 13:12-15, NASB). We have an example; now we must learn to live according to that example, and do as Christ has done for us. We must try to learn to walk straight and live straight before we set about instructing others.

A PHILOSOPHIC BALDPATE

Once upon a time a bald-headed man who wore a wig went for a ride on his horse. A gust of wind came along and blew the wig off his head, and all the people standing by began to laugh. As the man brought his horse to a stop, he said, "It's no wonder that I can't keep hair which isn't mine on my head, since its real owner, on whose head it once grew, couldn't keep it there either."

The moral of the story is: "A person should not be upset by the accidents which happen to him. What Nature did not give us at the time of our birth can never be a permanent possession. For naked we came into this world, and naked we shall leave."

FOUR YEARS AFTER I left my first parish, I returned to visit with friends of old in Nebraska. Some former parishioners whom I had not seen for a number of years immediately remarked, "Well, you haven't changed much except that you've lost a little more hair!" This was a friendly enough greeting except for the fact that people sometimes forget that ministers are sensitive about such subjects. I had not noticed in my present charge that I had been losing some hair. It had disappeared bit by bit and it had been a rather casual and unnoticed loss. It had never really been a concern before, but now that it was brought to my attention, I became quite self-conscious about the fact, particularly since I have not achieved that state of distinction which merits the wearing of another man's head of hair, as was the case with Aesop's horseman.

But I would remind you that Aesop's horseman was not the first philosophic baldpate in history. The Bible recounts that unusual story of an Old Testament character named Job, a man unlike any other man on earth. This man Job was upright, blameless, and filled with the fear of God. He constantly turned away from evil, and if that were not enough he was also a rich man who owned seven thousand sheep, three thousand camels, five hundred yoke of oxen and five hundred she-asses, as well as having a very great household. Job was a wealthy man even by our own present-day inflationary standards. But not only was he rich in the things of this world; he was also wealthy as a father, the head of a family and the royal priest of his household. He was a father who was proud of his sons and daughters, and they in turn surrounded him with their love.

It might seem to us today that Job was hedged in on all sides by God's blessings. It is no surprise then that Satan said, "No wonder he loves God. He has no reason *not* to love God. But just let me touch some of these blessings and let us then see if he does not curse God." So Satan, knowing the price of every camel, every lamb, and every yoke of oxen, now ponders the price on the head of this man Job. How many of his blessings will he have to lose before he will curse God? This was not an idle question on the lips of Satan, for he had tried other men and he knew that all men had a price. Now, like a tiger stalking his prey, Satan enters into the life of Job and begins to search for an opening, a weak spot where he might first attack his adversary. Satan knew the effects of poverty and pain. He knew the effects of the loss of prestige and power upon men. He knew how piety passes with personal losses, so that when some men are dethroned socially they become downhearted religiously. Then Satan, who felt that Job's love of God was a matter of circumstances, began to destroy the whole of Job's fortunate human situation.

But Satan totally misunderstood the nature of this man Job. Satan totally underestimated the love of God which Job held in his heart. Yet, one day when Job was eating and drinking, a messenger came and told him that his oxen and asses had been captured by enemies who also slew Job's servants with their swords. While he was still trying to comprehend this unfortunate piece of news, another man came and told him that fire from God had fallen and burned up his sheep and the servants who were tending them. While this man was yet speaking, another servant came and told him that the Chaldeans had raided his camels and taken them and slain all his servants by their swords. Were this not tragedy enough, he then heard that his sons and daughters had just been killed by a great wind. Now Job stood alone in the world.

Then Job arose, rent his robe, shaved his head, and fell upon the ground worshiping God saying, "Naked I came from my mother's womb, naked I shall return. The Lord gave and the Lord hath taken away. Blessed be the name of the Lord!"

Surely Job's philosophy proved that it is foolishness for a man to believe that he is safe from the temptation to curse God simply because of his environment. He was wiser perhaps than many today who feel that they are not tempted to deny the Lord their God, because of the comfortable circumstances in which they live. It was Job who showed us that circumstances are nothing more than temporary arrangements on God's earth and that man is not what he possesses but what he is.

We stand in awe and admiration of this man Job and his almost fanatical zeal to love God. But then, we too have seen people who have lost all their possessions in this world and they continue to love God, and we are tempted to say as Satan did answer God, saying, "Skin for skin, yea, all that a man hath will he give for his life. But put forth thine hand now, and touch his bone and his flesh, and he will curse thee to thy face" (Job 2:4-5).

How often we have heard this in the corridors and sickrooms of hospitals. "If a man has his health, he has everything." Satan, knowing well this human saying, said, "Touch the health. Touch his skin and bones and then see if he continues to love you!" Who knows? Maybe Job was just smart enough to have made a strategic retreat in this, his first encounter. Maybe his devotion to God was no more than lip service, giving him time to restore his properties again.

Now Satan tests Job again. The Lord afflicted Job with loathsome sores from the soles of his feet to the crown of his head. So horrible was this disease that Job was forced to go outside the city gates and sit in the city dump in the dung heaps where his only companions were the wild dogs and jackals! (At least when our flesh and bones are touched we have the comfort of a hospital bed and twenty-four-hour nursing care.) Still, even in this total distress, Job cried out his praises unto God. He still held fast to his love of God, refusing to curse God but trusting in His providential goodness and ultimate mercy.

Then Job's wife came to him and said, "Do you still hold fast to your integrity, Job? Why don't you curse God and die?" How Job's wife survived all the tragic blows that affected his household is beyond my understanding, unless she was spared that she might continue to plague him with her nagging presence. But now, even in the face of her shrill voice, Job continued to praise God with his lips, saying, "The Lord gives and the Lord takes away. Blessed be the name of the Lord."

These ancient words of Job should speak to us today with double strength. Our age is an age which is beginning to cautiously question and examine the possibility of God's sovereignty. Job cried out in faith, "I know that my God lives and reigns over this world." What Job so plainly said in Old Testament language is carried over into the New Testament in the life and teaching of Jesus Christ, and fulfilled in that final revelation of Saint John. There in the last book of the New Testament, the imprisoned visionary cries out, "Hallelujah! for the Lord reigns." God, who brought us into this world, will watch over us and guide us until we depart from it. Regardless of the circumstances, God shall continually be our strength and our refuge. This is the first lesson to learn.

The second lesson that Job teaches us comes in answer to the rather current controversy which is somewhat blithely called the new morality. As theology is gradually beginning to feel its way into what has been termed "situation ethics,"

Job, in his provincial faith, cried out, "Man's earthly situation makes no difference at all. Faith in God is faith in God. Naked we come into the world and naked we shall leave." We who feel that our situation entitles us to variants in moral behavior might well refer back again to the wise words of this philosophic baldpate, "Naked I came into the world, naked I shall leave." And now, clothed or naked, bald or wavy-haired, young or old, in love and honor, in duty and in service, in all faith and tenderness, in plenty and in want, in sickness and in health, in joy and in sorrow—and even in death—we are God's.

BIRDS OF A FEATHER

Once upon a time there was a man who intended to buy a donkey. He took it home on trial and put it into the corral with his own donkeys. The new donkey turned its back to all of the donkeys except one, which was the laziest and the greediest of the whole lot. The new donkey stood close beside the lazy one and did nothing. So the man put the bridle back on the donkey, took it to its owner, and told the man that he had decided not to buy it. "I am sure," he said, "that this donkey is just like the one that it singled out for a companion in my corral."

The moral of the story is: "A man's character is judged by the company that he keeps."

SEVERAL HUNDRED YEARS after Aesop had written his fables, a Greek comic poet and dramatist named Menander wrote much the same thought in his comedy entitled *Thais*. In the richness of practical wisdom it stated "Bad company ruins good morals." And as Menander borrowed from Aesop in thought, so also the apostle Paul might have borrowed from Menander in his thoughts. In his letter to the Corinthian church, Paul admonished those members of that early church, "Do not be deceived—bad company ruins good morals." The apostle Paul knew full well that there comes a time when a person must bid farewell to the company he is keeping, since he is being influenced by them more than he is able to influence them. He also knew that the natural education imbedded in the individual can rarely be prolonged beyond the years of adolescence. The time also arrives in the course of human growth when the home ceases to be an exclusive influence in the formation of character. It is succeeded by the more artificial education of the school and even more completely by the companionship of friends and comrades who mold the character by the powerful influence of personal example.

It is because of the power of this personal example that many men, young and old, imitate those with whom they associate. We are all imitators by nature, and we are all more or less impressed by the speech, the manners, gestures, and habits of our closest companions. Imitation, though it be ever so unconscious, affects the whole course of life by the permanence of its influence. We are reminded that, though the strong often impress the weak, even the weakest natures exercise some influence on those around them. Simply being together, simply the approximation of feeling, of thought, and of constant action yield a certain amount of imitation.

It was Emerson who made the wise observation that all couples who have grown old together through the years seem to grow gradually to become like one another, so that if their lives were extended through time, and should they live long enough, it would be almost impossible to tell them apart. If this is true of the old, how much more is it true of those who are young, whose plastic natures are so much softer and so much more impressionable, ready to take the stamp of the life and the conversations of those round about them?

Here I must confess my uncontrollable habit of people watching. Living as close as I do to a high school, it is virtually impossible to avoid noticing the daily parade of students who plod past on our sidewalks each morning as they go to school, and who bounce by later in the afternoon as they leave the school. It is impossible not to notice that they all dress in a similar fashion and that to a degree they all act in a similar fashion. They all walk in a similar fashion, and where there is any noticeable divergence from the norm, the differing student is usually accompanied or surrounded by a group of his peers in various stages of differentiation from the usual pattern.

I must confess that I marvel at their desire to conform, to be exactly like their companions, to imitate the norm. I must force myself at times to remember that each young person in that passing parade possesses in himself the power of his own will and of his own free activity which he could rightly exercise. But I wonder if perhaps they have given up all their own inclinations and given themselves unto a servile imitation of others. Then in remembering the saying "birds of a feather flock together," I often make certain basic judgments about the character of students I do not know, by my knowledge of the character of their associates and friends. With Aesop's consent, I say to myself, "A man's character is judged by the company he keeps."

Here, I feel that you are ready to remind me that we are all imitators, and so in the same breath let me answer with the admonition which Paul set before the congregation at Corinth. Paul reminds those people that we are unable to escape the moral and the psychological consequences of the fact that we are members one of another. All the subtle and pervading influences of our total human environment affect each one of us every day. Therefore, Paul reminds us that we should associate with people who are wiser, better, and more experienced than we are ourselves. Paul is not so much saying that there are people with whom we should not associate as he is saying that there are people with whom we would do well to associate. We should find in their lives something invigorating and something inspiring for our lives. We should allow them to enhance our knowledge of life. We should correct our estimates of some of life's experiences by the richness of their experiences, and at the same time become partners with them in wisdom. We should enlarge the field of our observations through their eyes, not only from what they have enjoyed, but also to profit from the experiences wherein they have suffered.

Paul said, "Do not be deceived. Bad company ruins good morals." Though the age of moralistic preaching may have passed with the death of the apostle Paul, it still holds true that our actions seem less evil when they are placed alongside the actions of others with similar desires and inclinations.

However, we should not be warned of the dangers of bad company without being instructed in the value of good companionship. Let us now turn this maxim around. Instead of being overly concerned about keeping ourselves pure and undefiled in a sinful world by avoiding the world, let us examine instead the possibility of being living examples of the power of Christ's love in the world. Let us, with the knowledge that Christ is our constant strength, consider the possibility of being Christ's witnesses. Let us be constant examples of His gospel in whatever company we keep. Let us see if we can, in some way, invest ourselves into this world of which we are a part so that we become an influence upon others, letting our lives influence the environments in which we live, not deserting the world because it is the world. It was for this reason that Jesus talked to tax collectors and sinners, for to eat with sinners meant to choose them as friends and companions with whom one would "break bread." To Christ there were no hopeless souls. As God seeks us in our lostness, we now need to seek others in their lostness. As much as we are concerned about becoming involved in the company of all God's people, we should not be overly concerned with retreating from that company which is less than God's desire for mankind, that we might be a light unto them. Let us become influences of Christ's love to the world and an example and witness of the gospel which is the salvation of mankind.

To be sure, the admonition which Paul presented to that Corinthian congregation has bearing and validity to all of us today. Be well reminded of the fact that, in ourselves, we are not so strong that we can long endure the temptations of this world. We must remind ourselves, as Paul reminded the Corinthians, that constant exposure to the temptations of this world will leave us weak-kneed and most susceptible to the accusations of not living according to our faith. This judgment pronounced upon us does carry with it a certain inherent danger. But the judgment is not as important as the fact that the power of others over us may quite unnoticeably change and affect our lives. Paul is simply reminding us that we stand in constant danger of losing the freedom to be our best selves for Christ. We can lose freedom to develop ourselves into the highest powers available to us. We are also reminded that even with this inherent danger we cannot and we must not forsake the world. We should be able, by the grace of God, to grow in faith and in courage to that point where, as mature adults, we can put away the dangers of youthful passions and become good company for the whole world!

THE CONCERN IS COMMITMENT

Once upon a time a man and a satyr (which is half man, half animal) struck up an acquaintance. In the evening they sat down together to eat. Since the day was very cold, the man put his fingers to his mouth and blew on them.

"Why did you do that?" asked the satyr.

"Well," said the man, "my hands were so very cold that I wanted to warm them up." It was not long before the waiter brought some hot food and put it before them. Then the man raised the dish to his mouth and blew on his food.

"Well now," said the satyr, "Why did you do *that?*"

"Oh," answered the man, "my food is so hot that I blew on it to cool it off."

"Ah-ha," said the satyr. "As of this moment, I renounce our friendship. I will have nothing to do with a man who can blow hot and cold with the same breath."

The moral of the story is: "To be both for and against makes no friends on either side."

IT IS NOT SO EASY for us to dissociate ourselves from men who blow hot and cold with the same breath. There are altogether too many men who arrange their thoughts to meet variant situations with various points of view. There are men who are simultaneously for integration and segregation, for war and against war, for the government's foreign policy and against the government's foreign policy, who would die for the truth that God is alive, but who live as though God were dead. There are men and women who can sit through countless church and civic committee meetings without making any enemies on either side of any controversy. They are able to blow both hot and cold, depending upon the prevailing mood of the committee. Such fence-sitters often become committee chairmen. It is in light of this fact that we have the saying today that a camel is a horse designed by a committee whose chairman did not want to offend any of the members and refused to take a stand himself.

As Christians, we cannot afford the false luxury of fence-straddling. We must take a stand in the life of the church. We must, in the life of the church, come to grips with the commitment which we have made for Christ. The concern of the church, the body of Christ, is this commitment. The constant concern of the church has always been commitment. The repeated challenge of the Old Testament was that picture of man constantly being confronted with alternate choices and challenges in life. He had to choose between God and mammon, between the present and the future, between good and evil.

Joshua, who led the children of Israel into Jericho, concludes the long exodus march with a farewell address in which he reminds the people of the mighty acts of God toward them. Then he challenges them to choose the Lord as their God. Joshua concludes his magnificent address saying, "If you be unwilling to serve the Lord, choose you this day whom you will serve. The gods of your fathers in the regions beyond the river, the gods of the Amorites in whose lands you dwell. Choose whom you will. But as for me and my house, we will serve the Lord" (Jos 24:15). The people responded with one cry, saying, "We also will serve the Lord for He is our God." But even then Joshua was not completely satisfied, for he knew that God was a jealous God whose commands demanded steadfast obedience. Therefore he made one final plea, reminding the people that they could not serve the Lord their God and other gods. They could not blow hot and cold at the same time. They could not be half for God and half against Him. The concern was for commitment, total commitment. In quick answer to this plea, the people put away all their other gods and they dedicated themselves anew to the Lord God of Israel.

The children of Israel were not faithful to their commitment, and by the time of the prophet Elijah, the people had acquired new gods. Once again they found themselves unable to distinguish between the false gods of Baal and the true God of Israel. Once more they found themselves blowing hot and cold with the same breath, diluting the words of God with the false words of the prophets of Baal. Then Elijah, in his despair, came to all the people as they gathered at Mount Carmel. He said, "How long will you go limping between two different opinions? If the Lord is God, then follow Him; but if Baal is god, then follow after him" (1 Ki 18:21). You cannot serve two Gods at the same time.

There are some occasions in life where you simply cannot straddle the fence, and this was one of them. Man must, at some time, commit his life completely either to one side or to the other. A kingdom divided falls into desolation. A

house divided falls into ruin. A man divided falls into a
death more pitiful than the pains of human death. A man
simply cannot let two Gods rule over his life anymore than
he can let two opposing passions direct his existence.

Such schizophrenic action ultimately destroys the human
soul. Those who have read Hawthorne's *Scarlet Letter* will
understand the impossibility of any man surviving in such
schizoid patterns. The pitiable deterioration of the personality of the Rev. Mr. Dimmesdale comes to a full reali-
zation in the twentieth chapter when Hester has secured
passage aboard a departing vessel. In light of the minister's
changing personality, the author states, "No man, for any
considerable period, can wear one face to himself, and another to the multitude, without finally getting bewildered as
to which may be the true."

Jesus knows the heart of man, and He knows well that
no human being can be a faithful servant of God, and at the
same time be a servant of anything that opposes God. Jesus
suffered through this same type of experience in the wilderness when the tempter came to Him in an effort to thwart
the divine plan of redemption. Yet in spite of all that the
tempter could offer, Jesus, in the climactic conclusion of the
challenge, turned to Satan and said, "Get thee hence, Satan:
for it is written, Thou shalt worship the Lord thy God, and
him only shalt thou serve" (Mt 4:10). The whole world
was offered as a prize, and yet Jesus knew that He could not
divide His commitment to God's will.

It may well have been out of this experience that later,
in speaking to His disciples one day, Jesus said to them,
"No servant can serve two masters; for either he will hate
the one, and love the other, or else he will hold to one, and
despise the other. You cannot serve God and Mammon"
(Lk 16:13, NASB). No man can blow hot and cold with

the same breath anymore than a man can be a slave to two different masters at the same time. In either case he renders himself an incomplete being and thus of service to neither master nor to himself.

There are some simple laws in life and this surely is one of them. A man cannot walk east and west at the same time. A man cannot blow hot and cold with the same breath, and neither can he serve two masters at the same time. Nor can man serve God and at the same time serve that which is opposed to God. The concern is for commitment; not partial commitment, but total commitment, an unwavering and an unswerving commitment to Christ as the Lord of life. This is what He demands of us.

Therefore, to those who find no joy in Jesus Christ, to those who find no satisfaction in the Scriptures, to those who find no comfort in the church of Christ, to those who find no grace in the gospel, let me suggest that it may be because you have not given it that priority in your life which it demands. It may be that your life is so divided that even you have become bewildered as to which is the ruling passion of your existence.

Hear once more the call which is proclaimed throughout the church of Jesus Christ, a concern which is expressed for the total commitment of your life. We must say again, with the prophets of old, "Choose you this day whom you will serve." No man can serve two masters at the same time, no man can walk east and west at the same time, and no mouth can blow hot and cold with the same breath.

NATURE'S PUNISHMENT OF DISCONTENT

Once upon a time there were hawks who had singing voices as clear and as lovely as the bluebird. But when the hawks heard the neighing of the horses in the field beside them, they were very envious and did their best to imitate the horses. In trying to learn this new sound, the hawks lost the beautiful voices they already possessed. They could not learn to neigh like horses, and they also forgot how to sing.

The moral of the story is: "Contentment lies not in acquiring what is desired, but in using what is possessed."

TO BE DISCONTENT with what we have in our desire to have something else seems to be the history of mankind. Sigmund Freud left us a great body of literature dealing with some of our cultural problems. One of the finest of his later writings is *Civilization and Its Discontents* wherein Freud states, "The impression forces itself upon one that men measure by false standards, that everyone seeks power, success, riches for himself and admires others who attain them, while undervaluing the truly precious things in life."

The general pervasiveness of this vague feeling of discontent which is so much a part of our culture should give us some cause for concern. Its genesis is rooted in the very violation of the tenth commandment, "Thou shalt not covet." We find it almost impossible to believe that we, in this most affluent society, could possibly be guilty of the violation of this commandment. However, this law stands as one of man's earliest insights, the knowledge that our hidden desires in life quickly determine the nature of our destiny. The evil that men do is long before accomplished in their hearts and minds. It was this commandment which precipitated the very words of Jesus Christ when He said, "For from within, out of the heart of men, proceed evil thoughts, . . . covetousness, wickedness. . . . All these evil things come from within, and defile the man" (Mk 7:21). Thus the Stoics of Jesus' day may well have had some knowledge of the truth when they said, "If you want to make a man happy, add not to his possessions, but take away from his desires."

As in the Old Testament so also in the New Testament we read again and again that it is not the rich but those who desire to be rich who fall into temptation. It is this desire which opens the sluice gates through which pour out all the other harmful and hurtful desires which prevent men from realizing the fulfillment of their destiny.

Likewise, when Jesus sent His disciples forth into the world He also uttered a plea that they might be free from any anxiety over material possessions. Not, mind you, that they would be free from material possessions, but that they would be freed from the anxiety about them!

Consequently, when Paul informed the members of that parish in Philippi that he had learned to be content in whatever state he was in, he admitted to a far higher state of grace than many of us can possibly pretend today. If there is one theme song which I believe would characterize the nature of the world today, it would be the wailing chant of discontent. The discontent of husbands with their wives and wives with their husbands, parents with their children and children with their parents, teachers with their students and students with their teachers, neighbors with their neighbors, employers and employees, producers and consumers, the old and the young, the constant complaint of those who desire the authority, the power, the wealth, the techniques, the prestige, the talent, and the advantages possessed by others.

So it was no small achievement when the apostle Paul said, "I have learned in whatsoever state I am, therewith to be content." The word for "content" that the apostle Paul uses here is not used elsewhere in this, its strictest translation. By *content,* Paul means that he has learned to become self-sufficient or undefeated, not captured by the circumstances of life or enraptured by the circumstances of others.

By no means is this a text which the rich can apply to the poor. For that is the kind of interpretation which forces the poor to drink the vinegar of the cross and then smack their lips as though they found it to be as refreshing as wine. Notice here that the apostle Paul is not saying that he is content with what he is; he is instead saying that he is content with what he has!

I believe that the apostle Paul at this ripe age in life has a certain prerogative to say something about what he has. Let us consider his present condition. First, he was not a wealthy man. At this point he was so poor that he received a gift of charity from the church that he had founded. He was not a rich man speaking to the poor, but a poor man speaking to those who were helping him. Behind the fact of his present poverty stood the memory of his former wealth.

However, not only was his financial situation grim, but his physical situation was even more depressing. For he was writing from prison, chained to a Roman soldier, like a caged bird with eager wings beating in vain against the bars of his imprisonment. At that point he wrote: "I have learned in whatsoever state I am, therewith to be content."

We ought to shudder when, in our freedom to proclaim the gospel without any restrictions, we should find excuses and murmur in discontent at the weight of the burden that has been placed upon us. Both in the days when he was rich and in the days when he was poor, Paul knew how to remain content in whatever state he happened to be. Paul knew how to live humbly and he knew how to live in prosperity, and the latter was perhaps the most difficult of the two. As Thomas Carlyle once said, "For one man who can stand prosperity, there are a hundred who can stand adversity."

It is possible that through Paul we may be guided into this knowledge, which is in Christ Jesus. It was through Christ that the apostle Paul received this new perspective on life. Paul acquired this glorious habit of contentment through practice and perseverance on his part. He reminds us that he was constantly aware of the fact that God was sovereign not only in his life, but also in the world. Whether a man was being cast into the depths of sorrow or being raised into the raptures of the visions of heaven, Paul knew that in either case it was only according to God's appointment, and His sovereign will. Paul knew that there was no moving thing upon the face of this earth whose very sustenance, whose very being, whose very nourishment did not depend upon God. Paul also knew that his life should be in dependence upon God, and that God had a will for that life. So Paul busied himself in worshiping God and cut off all covetousness of anything else. Paul relied upon God as his sufficiency and his guardian. Paul's contentment was not through any power or any will of his own, not in his own self-sufficiency, but only in the fact that God would provide that which would be sufficient for him.

Furthermore, Paul found his contentment in *being* rather than in *having* or doing. Having all the possessions in the world would have been of no avail at all to Paul as he sat there in his prison cell. His contentment was in his union, his being with God. Augustine likewise said in his *Confessions,* "Our hearts are restless until they find their rest in Thee." So Paul found the meaning of contentment in the union of his spirit with the spirit of God. It is for this reason that Paul in his many epistles and letters constantly writes of being "in Christ."

Lastly, Paul has made that great discovery that his confidence and his strength are not in himself but in the sustaining strength and power of Jesus Christ. We begin adult life with great confidence in our own natural abilities and strength, but as we grow in age and in wisdom, we find ourselves growing not stronger and stronger but weaker and weaker, until at last we avail ourselves of the strength of God. It is then that we learn our strength is not in ourselves but in Jesus Christ. In that knowledge, may we find our own contentment.

MOTE AND BEAM

Once upon a time, it is said by the Greeks, Prometheus fashioned all men and hung two small bags from their necks. The bag in front contained all the defects and faults of other people, and the bag in back contained all their own faults and defects. Thus it was said that men were able to see their neighbor's faults a mile away, but they were never able to perceive their own.

The moral of the story is: "A man should be careful about concerning himself with other men's sins when he is blind in regard to his own."

IT IS NOT OUR RESPONSIBILITY to examine each other, but to examine ourselves. To examine each other would be no difficult task. Every man is prone to rearrange the true character of others in his own mind. Even the disciples must have reflected at times upon their own peculiar relationship with Christ and each other, perhaps even as they gathered together and celebrated the Last Supper.

Simon Peter sitting at the Lord's Supper that night glances to his right and sees Andrew, the most conservative of the disciples—Andrew, who always did the proper thing at the proper time. Simon Peter wonders how such a conservative and cautious creature of God came to be a disciple of the unconventional Jesus!

At the same time, Andrew glances to his left and sees Peter looking at him, yet beyond him, and he wonders to himself how such a reckless rogue, such a radical thinker, such a frank and outspoken man, could possibly carry on as a disciple of the meek and humble Jesus!

John the Beloved, sitting at the right hand of Christ, glances down to the end of the table and sees James, his brother, gray-haired, wearied, apparently much too old to be of any real service in this new kingdom to which they constantly referred. James in turn looks at John and wonders how such a young man can possibly carry on after the death of the Master. Much too young! Much too emotional! So lacking in the wisdom of years and the stability of maturity.

Philip, leaning back in his chair, sees James and Andrew and Judas listening intently to Nathanael. Looking into the glistening eyes of Nathanael, Philip wonders how such a profound thinker, a man with such a sense of humor, such quick wit, and yet possessing such a keen intellect, could possibly be included among the followers of the prosaic and common Christ. Nathanael in turn looks at Philip, sitting there in all his pious laziness, and wonders how such a dull laggard, such a slow-witted plodder, such a gullible Greek, could possibly carry on as a follower of the profound and poetic Jesus.

At the left end of the table Matthew is talking to Jude and Simon. As he talks he gesticulates in a wild manner, using his hands more than his voice. In fact he almost hits Thomas at his right with his wild gestures! And Thomas, pausing for a moment and saying nothing, looks at Matthew's hands— hands that used to gather in the taxes of the oppressed—and Thomas wonders how such a man—a publican, despised as the oppressor of his own people, an outcast from Israel— could possibly be a follower of this Jesus of Nazareth.

But Matthew, a man of fearless faith who rose up at the word of the Lord and followed Him, is now through speaking. He turns to Thomas and apologizes for the disturbance he has created. But looking closely at Thomas, he wonders to himself how a man of such skeptical intellect, who constantly blinked in unbelief, could possibly hope to be a source of faith and strength to others.

As the servants bring in the supper, James the Just looks about to make sure that all are served. He motions to Jude to see that Simon, at the end of the table, receives his due portion. And James wonders for a minute about Jude—the theologian, the man of doctrine. Does he not realize that morality and righteousness are also important? How can a man be so blind and still be a follower of Christ?

Jude, having served Simon, passes the plate back to James. Jude wonders for a minute about James—the moralist, so concerned with keeping every letter of the law. Does not James realize that mere morality isn't enough? Does he not remember that we are to serve God with our minds as well as with public deeds of righteousness? How can a man be so blind and still be a follower of Christ?

Then Simon, having finished all that Jude had given him to eat, looks up from his plate and meets the dark eyes of Judas, the businessman. Judas, who counts all things, who keeps track of all things, who balances the budget, but who lacks the zealous enthusiasm of an adventurer for Christ. And Simon the Zealot mutters his own personal vow again: "Christ first at any cost! Let me suffer the loss of all things, but let me win Christ!"

And there they were, gathered around the Lord's Table, even as we often gather about the Lord's Table to celebrate the holy sacrament. What do we see as we look around at one another? We see what they saw. But by the grace of God, we are not asked to measure another fellow's faults. Instead the commandment of the New Testament to each of us is: "Let every man examine *himself*, . . . and then let him eat of that bread and drink of that cup" (1 Co 11:28). Jesus put it this way: "Why beholdest thou the mote that is in thy brother's eye, but perceivest not the beam that is in thine own eye?" (Lk 6:41).

UNITY IS STRENGTH

Once upon a time there was a father whose sons were always fighting with each other. The father tried to persuade them to mend their ways, but he found that his words were not making any impression upon them. One day he asked them all to bring him a stick. Then he tied all the sticks together into a bundle and one by one he asked his sons to try to break it. Try as they would, they were not able to break it. Then he untied the bundle and gave the sticks back one at a time. Now they were able to break each stick very easily. So the father said, "You see, my children, it will be the same with you. As long as you stand together, no enemy will ever overcome you. But if you quarrel and fight among yourselves, you will be an easy victim for others."

The moral of the story is: "Men are vulnerable when divided, but it is in their union that they find their strength."

ON THE TWENTIETH OF JUNE in 1966, Charles DeGaulle
carried the greetings of the people of Paris to the people of
Moscow. A member of one of the NATO nations carried
greetings to one of the members of the Warsaw Pact nations
in the hope of reestablishing Europe as a fertile whole instead of the paralyzed parts then existing in sterile division.
As wars continue to be waged on the opposite side of the
world, Europeans are beginning to understand that even
though they have been at loggerheads with each other for
centuries, they will soon have to mend their ways if they
expect to maintain any degree of invulnerability. With some
degree of wisdom, they are beginning to realize that their
reunion will make them strong, and that their divisions simply supply the tinder which might conceivably ignite into
another European holocaust.

Charles DeGaulle attempted to do in Europe in 1966
exactly what the United States failed to do at the end of the
Second World War. At that time we united different member nations of God's world into various pacts and treaties,
thinking that perhaps strength would counterbalance
strength. Thus, we hoped that this world would for some
time be able to live in peace. We would have been wiser if
we had gone back to the words of one of our own Presi-
dents, Abraham Lincoln, who in his debates with Stephen
Douglas in the year 1856, gave his famous "House Divided"
speech. Lincoln described the total impossibility of this
country ever enduring as long as it was half slave and half
free. In a brilliant summation of the political and social
structure of the world of his day, Lincoln said, "If a house
is divided against itself, the house will not be able to stand."
So many school boys and girls have learned that speech by
heart that they have since come to associate it with the mind
of Abraham Lincoln. But Lincoln knew then what the

church is just beginning to discover today. These words spoken by Christ our Lord were meant not as poetic ideals, but as a basis of human conduct and concern.

It is good today to see the quest for unity on the international scene. It is heartening to see evidence of Christ's words being taken seriously on the national scene. But the question which bears a burning regard for us centers on the local scene. We who would like to live in a world of peaceful alliances and fruitful relationships must first learn to establish these marks of unity in our own lives.

At times I think that mediating family quarrels among children is equally as difficult as solving the problems of a divided nation. Since our subjective involvement is equally divided between both dissenting parties among our own children, it becomes extraordinarily difficult to mete out any form of objective justice. Knowing that the writer of the Psalms had his family problems too, we can empathize with the depth of his emotions when he wrote, "Behold, how good and how pleasant it is for brethren to dwell together in unity . . . for there the LORD commanded the blessing, even life for evermore" (Ps 133:1, 3*b*).

David knew something about brothers dwelling in unity. He also knew something about brothers who did not dwell in unity. David, who had become weakened by his own sins, remembered well the problems which he had in disciplining his own sons. He remembered the misery of discovering that his life had become so wretched and entangled in sin that it embarrassed him to correct the faults of his children. Therefore he chose to overlook their disunity rather than to correct that which was causing them to be divided; for they were, in their sins, doing exactly what he was doing in his divisiveness against God.

David knew about the sin of Ammon against his sister

Tamar. He knew that the sin had gone unpunished. He knew at that moment the seriousness of the division in his own household, but he also felt that there was nothing that he could do about it. This division made his children vulnerable, not only to attacks from without but also to attacks from within. It was not long before Ammon's brother Absalom began to harbor a hatred for Ammon which was uncontrollable. It was a smoldering resentment which in time fanned itself into a raging fire consuming his every passion. At last in an opportune moment, Absalom took justice into his hands and murdered Ammon, his brother. The over-imaginative rumor-mongers of that day, knowing that David was already worried about the divisions within his house, carried the word to him that Absalom had slain Ammon and all his brothers. At this crucial moment in the life of David's family when he should have taken action to heal the division which was growing in his own home, he sat back paralyzed with vacillating intentions refusing to heal the breach which soon would become the opening sluice gates of revolt.

Absalom, now realizing that the division of the house was a fact, also realized that he had suddenly become a very vulnerable man. So he sought his own union that he might be strong. He got himself horses and chariots and fifty men to run before him. Then he would arise early in the morning and stand by the gates of the city. There he would greet the travelers from the tribes of Israel and promise them justice if they would follow him. Thus he won their hearts to his cause. Soon Absalom's strength was such that he began to consider the possibility of unseating his father David from the throne of Israel. David, panic-stricken by the power of Absalom's forces, fled from the city with his six hundred bodyguards. As David fled from one gate, Absalom entered the other and occupied the city, violating his father's concubines, and thus making the division of the house of David complete!

But there was one more step before Absalom would have complete power over all Israel. That step demanded the death of David. It is at this point that Absalom hesitated. Though he desired his father's throne, he shrank back from the thought of being responsible for his death. But the course of history had moved beyond the bounds of self-concern and David and Absalom became engaged in all-out war, Absalom not wanting to kill David, and David instructing his soldiers to spare the life of Absalom. So the battle began. It was a battle that had its genesis years before in the home of David when his children began to fight against each other. In the course of the battle Absalom was killed. From David we hear that most pitiable lament of the whole Old Testament, "O my son Absalom, my son, my son Absalom! would God I had died for thee, O Absalom, my son, my son!" (2 Sa 18:33). Then David knew how good and pleasant it would have been if brothers had at one time learned to dwell in unity!

In the pages of the New Testament, Jesus reminds us once again of this ancient truth, saying, "If a kingdom is divided against itself, that kingdom cannot stand. And if a house is divided against itself, that house will not be able to stand" (Mk 3:24-25, NASB).

Perhaps we can now see something of the danger of those human divisions which alienate us one from another and from Jesus Christ our Lord. Let us therefore reaffirm our commitments to one another in the household of God and to Jesus Christ whom we serve, that thus united we may stand strong for His glory and praise.

A FRIEND IN NEED IS A FRIEND INDEED

Once upon a time there were two friends who were traveling along a road together. Suddenly a wild bear appeared before them. The one man climbed up into a tree and there he remained safely hidden. The other man, seeing that he was going to be caught before he had a chance to escape, lay down on the ground and pretended to be dead. The bear put his nose to the man on the ground and smelt him all over. The man held his breath and pretended to be dead, for he had heard that a bear will not touch a dead man.

Soon the bear went away and then the other man came down from the tree. He asked his friend what the bear had whispered into his ear while he was so close. "Well," he said, "the bear told me not to travel any more with a friend who doesn't stand by you in a moment of danger."

The moral of the story is: "Real friends are proven in times of adversity."

ONE OF THE MOST UNUSUAL RELATIONSHIPS recorded in the Old Testament is that which existed between Jonathan and David. Here was a friendship based on loyalty which crossed all social and political lines. Jonathan was Saul's son and the heir apparent to the throne. He was a popular prince, an able athlete, a handsome and courageous young man. It was this Jonathan who went into the wilderness to visit David. David had incurred the king's displeasure and he was now hiding in the darkness of disgrace. He was being hunted by Saul's soldiers from hut to hovel until no man dared to shelter him. David was wandering from sunrise to sunset in the stubble-strewn wilderness, and Jonathan went into the wilderness to strengthen David's hand in the Lord. Jonathan the prince went to David the outcast to give him hope and courage!

Granted, these two young men were not strangers. They had met before. Jonathan was there that day when David rocked Goliath to never-ending sleep. He was there to hear the wild and enthusiastic cheers of all the people. Thus, it takes no mental gymnastics to understand and believe that the soul of Jonathan was knit that day to the soul of David (1 Sa 18:1). But even a friendship so firmly knit can snag and unravel. How long, we might ask, should a friendship last? David was no longer the national hero he once was. David was a national enemy in the eyes of the king. We might have reminded Jonathan that as times change, friendships also are subject to change. How long is it necessary for a man to maintain a friendship, especially when such a relationship becomes strained through the loss of mutual friends? These are some of the thoughts that must have

been in Jonathan's mind. But if they were, he soon over-
came any doubts and misgivings he might have had, for he
quickly rose up and went to David in the woods, and strengthened his hand in the Lord. Jonathan knew that true friendship is loyal friendship. True friendship is proved by adversity.

Jonathan also knew that even beyond loyalty, a friendship
once established can only be maintained through love, sym-
pathetic love. You notice that Jonathan did not "say it with
flowers." He did not dispatch a team of trained evangelists
to David. He did not drop David a postcard (mimeo-
graphed) inviting him to come and have fellowship with
him. Not at all! Instead, he went to David himself and he
strengthened David's hand with his own hand. He talked
with him and he walked with him. Jonathan stepped down
from his princely balcony and went to David where David
was—in the woods.

Such a loving friendship exercised today would indeed be
a reflective motion for Christianity. It is this concern, manifest by relating ourselves mentally, physically, and spiritually
with our brothers, that knit the heart of Jonathan to David,
that bound Paul to Onesiphorous, that united the disciples
together in the early life of the church, and that has bonded
members together in the bosom of the church for centuries.
The miracle of strengthening a neighbor's hand in the Lord
is that we cannot honestly grip hands without having our
hearts also gripped. Our concern for others will in time
rise above our own petty desires, whims, fancies, ambitions,
and prejudices. It is in this manner that we become bound
together in the body of Christ held fast by that silver cord of
love.

Jonathan's visit also expressed the loftiness of his friendship. Jonathan's friendship rose above the petty desires of

personal selfishness. It would not have been at all difficult to excuse Jonathan if he had shown signs of jealousy instead of friendship. If you remember, Samuel had anointed David to be king. Legally the throne belonged to Jonathan. Now David was hiding in fear and confusion. He was on the verge of forsaking his high calling. Jonathan needed to say nothing at all and the throne would be his. All Jonathan needed to do was sit tight and wait for David's capture and decapitation. His legal worries would be over, and his regal worries as well! Instead, Jonathan deliberatly went into the woods to David. He restored David's faith and consequently Jonathan moved David coser to the kingly throne which might well have been his own. Jonathan's love for David surmounted the pitfalls of self-love and related itself to the love of God. Herein lies true friendship, that we can give ourselves to others through the love of God without seeking anything for ourselves in return.

In turning to the New Testament, let us consider another type of friendship—this time in a negative sense. One of the most interesting organizational aspects of Christ's ministry through His followers lies in His method of sending them forth into the world. We read in the gospels that He sent them forth "two by two" (Mk 6:7). His reliance was not in conferences, congresses, and conventions as much as it was in the constant influence of single companions, single friends. So it was that His followers went forth into the world two by two. We can only imagine how close these friendships must have become between these men paired off together. Even after His ascension, the principle continued, exemplified by Peter and John, Paul and Silas, Barnabas and Mark. Jesus affirmed the thesis that it is good for a man to walk with friends.

Yet it may have been better for one of the disciples,

Judas, if he had walked alone. The friendship of the other
eleven men did not reach out to him. Surely at times the
other disciples must have been aware of the thoughts that
were running through Judas' mind. Surely they were aware
of the doubts and the problems that lingered and soon
festered in Judas' heart. Why did they not help Judas? Why
did they not fulfill the responsibilities of friendship and tell
Judas some of the things that only a friend can say? Surely
in the heat of the day when they rested in the shade of the
trees, they could have spoken openly and honestly to Judas.
Surely on some of those warm summer nights as they slept
in the open looking up at the stars, they could have opened
their hearts to Judas. What manner of a friendship was this,
to let Judas drift so far from the heart of Christ?

But then, haven't we all missed the central meaning of
true friendship? Isn't this also the case with us? We see our
nearest and dearest friends doing some things that we know
are in contradiction to the will of God and yet we hesitate
to say anything. Why? Mainly because we are afraid of
making enemies out of friends. We are afraid that our
friends will no longer like us. Judas' companions probably
felt this way too. That may be one reason why they never
said anything to him. But look what happened to Judas.

Friends, true and false, are proven by adversity. Ours is
the task in Christian concern to maintain a loyal, loving,
and lofty friendship with others for Christ's sake. We are
our brothers' keepers, even in the hour of adversity and the
moments of despair. We must learn with Christ's help to
sustain and encourage one another, strengthening one another in the Lord, that at last it may be said of us:

Because of your firm faith, I kept the track
Whose sharp set stones my strength had almost spent—

I could not meet your eyes if I turned back,
  So on I went.

Because of your strong love, I held my path
When battered, worn and bleeding in the fight—
How could I meet your true blue eyes, blazing wrath?
  So I kept right.

AUTHOR UNKNOWN

THE EYE OF ENVY

Once upon a time all the animals gathered together in the forest. A monkey stood up in front of the other animals and danced and did some tricks. All the animals laughed and applauded the monkey's performance.

A camel who had watched it all grew jealous and also desired praise and attention. So the camel got up and tried to dance like the monkey, but he was such a ridiculous sight that all the other animals laughed and laughed. The camel was so embarrassed that he ran out of sight.

The moral of the story is: "Envy can make fools of us all."

THE MOST DIFFICULT PART of any vacation is returning home. Not that it is not exciting to see again the little village in the valley, and to anticipate again the camaraderie of old friends, but to begin again in the daily routine and to see

106

once more those things which are common and mundane and well-known lays the heart low with foreboding and apprehension instead of lifting it with joy. The stack of tasks left undone is now almost hidden under the voluminous pile of new tasks yet to be started. Muscles which rightly should be resiliently robust from relaxing rest tighten involuntarily. It becomes almost a fearful thing to step again upon the treadmill which we so recently left, and it is with caution that we take our first steps.

It is even more discouraging when upon returning home, you discover that your friends have caught fish immensely larger than the ones which you caught, that your neighbors traveled distances doubly farther than you did, that your colleagues climbed mountains measurably higher than the hills you climbed, and that your relatives whom you visited and who took you in are now coming to visit you. But this is as much a part of vacation as ants in the sugar and rain on the fire.

Why should a man be depressed when returning from a summer's trip? Why the constant cry in our hearts as we rest by the shore or in the mountains or by the lake, "Oh, if only I could just stay here"? Why the cry? It is no more than a touch of envy, a desire to be that which we are not, to have that which we have not.

The same story was in the very beginning. Eve looked upon the tree in the garden and perceived that the tree was good for food and a delight to the eyes. Because Adam and Eve desired that which was not theirs to have, they were driven from the garden. Envy and covetousness have been with us since that day.

The spirit of envy descends upon us so cleverly and insidiously, so slyly and treacherously. It creeps into our lives without our awareness or approval, and corrupts that which we once held dear. So easily does envy enter into our lives and so surreptitiously does it destroy our happiness that we are hardly aware of its presence. So it was with Saul in the Old Testament. After David had been appointed as a leader in the army, he became so successful that the people hailed him as a national hero. It was galling for Saul to hear the women singing, "Saul [has] slain his thousands, and David his ten thousands" (1 Sa 18:7). Envy grew in the heart of Saul, and Saul eyed David from that day on. He eyed him with the eye of envy, not the eye of appreciation, confidence, and patristic pride. He eyed him with envy, ever watching him and ever waiting to pounce upon him and destroy him. Thus Saul became incompetent in his own tasks. But David continued to win the hearts of the people and visions of David's greatness danced in the minds of the children of Israel. Then Saul was so frightened about his own status that he could not regard David with anything but fear. Saul struck out in all directions like a frightened animal, and in a moment of desperation, he sought to solve his problem by killing it.

Even within our experience, the problems which confront us are often the result of envy. The insecurity of the status seeker, the lethargy of the not-so-solvent businessman, the despair of the poor in worldly goods, and in our attempt to justify our own positions we do exactly as Saul did. We set out to destroy that which we cannot have and to minimize the value of that which we know will never be ours. But those who destroy often become so involved in destruction that they are unable to build. All the destructive wars in the world have never brought forth a permanent peace. And so it is that when man spends all his energies to destroy he rarely has strength left to build.

So Saul, in his feeble state, discovers that his envy has

turned into a pathological hatred and fear. He cannot keep his hate to himself and he betrays it to Jonathan. Even though Jonathan brings about a momentary reconciliation, it is apparent that such temporary palliatives are little more than useless. For to envy a man is to finally hate him! The hatred of Saul led him to search the corners of the land for David that he might destroy him, But instead of finding and destroying him, it was Saul who was destroyed, slain on Mount Gilboa. Envy and jealousy destroyed that which could have been a beautiful friendship, and at the same time caused Saul to made a ridiculous exhibition of himself.

You would think that Saul would have known the perils of jealousy simply through his knowledge of what happened during the wilderness experience of the Jews when Miriam and Aaron spoke out against Moses in a moment of jealousy. They said, "Has the Lord indeed spoken only through Moses? Has he not spoken through us also?" (see Num 12:2). Moses' sister, Miriam, was a prophetess in her own right, and when she noted that all Israel applauded Moses when he performed for the Lord, she became exceedingly jealous. Seeking equal praise, she instead brought ridicule and shame upon herself. God smote her with leprosy and she was driven outside the camp.

It may have been through this crucible of experience and the knowledge of perils past that the writer of Proverbs admonishes his readers, "Wrath is cruel, anger is outrageous; but who is able to stand before envy?" (Pr 27:4). In the pages of the New Testament, we see again the effect of envy upon the hearts of men. Two men, Jesus and Barrabas, stand before Pilate, the procurator of Judea. These two men had been condemned to death, but as was the custom at the feast of the governor, one of the two prisoners was to be released for the crowd. So when they had gathered,

Pilate said to the crowd, "Whom do you want me to release for you, Barrabas or Jesus?" He knew that it was out of envy that they had delivered the Christ unto him. Out of envy—what a strange reason this was! Who would envy Christ? Would it be because of His popularity with the people? His miraculous power to heal? His character or His being? Pilate knew what envy was, for it lurked even in his own breast. Because of the envy in their hearts, the crowd answered, "Give us Barrabas!"

But what of the envy in our own hearts? How can we divest ourselves of this peril? In his letter to the church of Corinth, which was divided in thought by jealousy and strife, Paul reminds those parishoners—as we might well be reminded—that the only cure for this problem is love. Paul said, "Love is not jealous" (see 1 Co 13:4). Only when we love to the point of seeking the best for others will we be able to overcome the tendency which is natural to man, namely to love himself. Only the love of Christ filling our hearts will drive out the self-love which we harbor within ourselves.

The desire for things which are not ours to have will destroy our entire being. The jealousy in our hearts will destroy friendship and render us incapable of fulfilling our tasks, and we will look foolish in our attempts to compete with others out of envy.

THE FAULT LIES NOT IN OUR STARS

Once upon a time there was a man who was very tired, having taken a long journey. He lay down to rest at the edge of a cliff and went to sleep. He was in great danger of rolling off the edge of the cliff when Dame Fortune appeared and woke him up.

"If you had fallen off this cliff, my friend," she said, "instead of blaming your own foolishness, you probably would have blamed me."

The moral of the story is: "The faults and misfortunes of this life do not always lie in the stars but often in our own actions."

RECENTLY I heard Dr. Viktor E. Frankl, professor of psychiatry and neurology at the University of Vienna and the successor to Sigmund Freud, lecture on the basic principles of logotherapy. I confess the speech did not excite me as much as meeting this famous psychiatrist who survived three concentration camps in Germany, including Auschwitz and Dachau.

What intrigued me more than all else was to hear of the philosophical acceptance of such suffering by the prisoners at Auschwitz. Dr. Frankl repeatedly stated that this was due to a strong feeling that fate was one's master and that one must not try to influence it in any way. The merciless beatings, the extreme cruelty, and finally death which came to the inmates of these concentration camps for not reaching the demanded quotas were mainly due to the fact that their captors did not provide the necessary tools and equipment.

Moses and the Israelites were in a similar situation. They also lacked the equipment necessary for meeting production demands. In that day, Moses said to Pharaoh, "There is no straw given unto thy servants, and they say to us, Make bricks: and, behold, thy servants are beaten; but the fault is in [your] own people" (Ex 5:16). So also at Dachau, slaves were willing to work, but without tools they were unable to bring forth the desired results. As they were beaten they may have repeated again the words of Moses in their hearts, saying under their breath to the guards that beat them, "The fault is in your own people!"

Other prisoners, in considering their plight, might have remembered the lamentations of Jeremiah who in his distress cried out, "Our fathers have sinned, and are not; and we have borne their iniquities. We [get] our bread with the peril of our lives" (Lam 5:7-9a). So also, men living in the midst of history's greatest persecution often found their solace for their own misfortunes in blaming the faults of their predecessors.

The danger of such a fatalistic attitude toward life is that one soon ignores the very challenge of life itself and thus simply vegetates and in a short time one dies. Die they did at Dachau, Auschwitz, Belsen, and throughout Europe.

What Dr. Frankl discovered in his death-camp experiences was basically a reformulation of the thought of Nietzsche, who said, "He who has a why to live for can bear with almost any how." We too agree that whenever a man has an understanding of the reason for his existence, then and then alone does he have the strength to bear the, nature of that existence.

It is here that we as Christians should find a great source of strength in the course of our lives. Christianity knows no destiny nor any fate which is not at the same time regulated by man's own free decision. We believe that man is never simply the product of certain inescapable, unalterable conditions and circumstances. On the contrary, man is constantly confronted with the necessity of deciding how he is to live in situations in which God in His providence has placed him.

To put such dogma into poetic terms, consider the words of Cassius, a conspirator with Brutus against Julius Caesar. Shakespeare tells how these two men pondered their destiny and the fate of a nation. They wondered why it was that Caesar had received all the worldly honor and praise. Then Cassius said:

> Why, man, he doth bestride the narrow world
> Like a Colossus; and we petty men
> Walk under his huge legs, and peep about
> To find ourselves dishonourable graves.
> Men at some time are masters of their fates:
> The fault, dear Brutus, is not in our stars,
> But in ourselves, that we are underlings.

We should also be reminded that when things do not go

as we want them to in this world, the fault is not always in the stars, but more often than not, in ourselves. It is fitting then that the last book of the New Testament, which is totally eschatological in content, pictures Jesus standing at the door knocking, saying, "If any one hears My voice and opens the door, I will come in to him, and will dine with him, and he with Me" (Rev 3:20, NASB). Throughout the whole New Testament there is a great emphasis placed upon man's personal response to the call of Jesus Christ. This response carries with it a personal and public admission of our sense of sin and our moral responsibility throughout all the days of our lives.

There is a danger in a life guided and molded by a sense of fatalism and determinism. It can lead to moral deterioration, decay, and death. We must grasp some sense of our personal responsibility to God and then come to grips with the existential problems of our own human situation. Many years ago, St. Augustine, while considering this very same problem of man's response to the will of God, reported that a group of monks, on being taken to task for their moral slothfulness into which their piety had degenerated, declared, "Why do you preach to us about our duties and exhort us to fulfill them, since it is not we who act, but God who works in us. Let our superiors simply point out our duties, but let them not reprove us when we are at fault; since we are such as God has foreseen and His grace has not been given us to do better." The moral and the spiritual irresponsibility of these monks is an example of the peril to the spiritual life which will arise from such a deterministic concept of redemption. Even spiritual men today need to be reminded that the fault is not always in their superiors!

But at last it is again the apostle Paul who gives us perhaps the clearest New Testament insight into this baffling problem of human existence. In his theological treatise to the Roman church Paul states, "We know that all things work together for good to them that love God, to them who are the called according to his purpose. For whom he did foreknow, he also did predestinate to be conformed to the image of his Son" (Ro 8:28). What Paul is saying is not that the world will automatically yield itself to those who love God, nor that their plight in life will be any different or better than the plight of others; but instead that God will cooperate in all things and in all events for good to those who love Him. Even the suffering of this present time can become a source of blessing. If we are left to our own resources, then suffering is likely to harden and to embitter us, but God and God alone can transform the power of evil circumstances to good uses. Like Joseph of old, who found himself tossed into a pit to die, we should retort with the wise observation that even what others mean for evil, God can put to good use.

Here we find man's freedom. As we enter into every situation in life we see that we are being confronted with a challenge. In our freedom, we must see, with God's help, a means of meeting that challenge, and by the grace of God and with the help of Jesus Christ, we must, in each human situation, discover that response which is consistent with our faith in God, for we are freely responsible to that faith.

Likewise we must also remember that when things do not go according to our plans, we are not to despair as others who have no hope. We are instead to understand that in God's purpose for history there is some good which can come forth even out of the world's greatest evil, and we are called to bear witness to that which is good.

I found this all hard to believe until I met a man who brought forth good out of such human evil as Auschwitz and Dachau. Let us then as Christians not trip over this theological stone of stumbling, but let us who know Jesus Christ commit ourselves again in trust to the Lord our God who ordains the affairs of men, and who at the same time empowers man with the freedom to respond.

CRYING WOLF TOO OFTEN

Once upon a time there was a shepherd boy who was very fond of playing practical jokes. He liked to drive his flock of sheep some distance away from the village and then scare the villagers by shouting for help, saying that wolves had attacked his sheep. Each time he did this the inhabitants of the village came running out in alarm—until they realized that the shepherd boy was laughing at them, and then they went back to their work. But one day some wolves did come and they got between the shepherd boy and his flock of sheep. Again he called out to his neighbors to help him, but they thought he was still up to his old tricks. They didn't even bother to look at him and he lost all his sheep.

The moral of the story is: "If we lie continually, the time will come when people won't even believe us when we tell the truth."

"WHAT A TANGLED WEB we weave, when first we practice to deceive!" But then, telling the truth is not so simple a matter either. Nor does it always untangle the problems of life. Honesty is more than moral character purely disciplined. It should also include a basic appreciation of human involvement in life's situations. Thus the more complex a man's life becomes, the more he is responsible for telling the truth and the more difficult it is for him to do it. That is, the further one advances in life and the deeper one becomes involved in life's problems, the more difficult it becomes to be honest, to tell the truth. Men discover as time goes by that truth-telling has not been what we might call an endearing virtue. Man is constantly confronted with the desire to evade life's tensions simply by lying. Very often lying is the easiest way out of an uncomfortable situation, and who has not been confronted with this temptation?

Micaiah, a prophet in the court of Jehoshaphat, king of Judah, knew something of this human weakness. In the third year of Jehoshaphat's reign, Ahab, the king of Israel, suggested that Judah and Israel unite to wage war against the Syrians. Jehoshaphat was as anxious as Ahab, but being a religious man, he sought the advice of his prophets. So all his prophets were brought before him, four hundred in all, and he asked them point-blank whether or not he should wage war. All four hundred prophets, knowing that he wanted to wage war, cried out in one voice, "Go up; for the LORD shall deliver it unto the hand of the king" (1 Ki 22:6*b*). Such a sudden assurance from four hundred people must have raised some suspicions in the heart of Jehoshaphat, and he asked Ahab if there was another prophet whom they might interrogate. Ahab probably wondered what the word of one man would be against the voice of four hundred, but he held back his thoughts and said, "There is yet one man,

Micaiah, the son of Imlah, by whom we may enquire of the LORD: but I hate him: for he doth not prophecy good concerning me, but evil" (1 Ki 22:8). Then Jehoshaphat demanded to hear the prophecy of Micaiah, and a servant was dispatched to fetch the prophet. Fortunately, the servant happened to be one of Micaiah's friends and he warned Micaiah of the words said by the king, as well as telling him what the other prophets had proclaimed. Thus Micaiah, knowing that the king ought not wage war against Ramoth-Gilead, faced a difficult situation.

First, he stood as one man against four hundred. His advice would be weighed against the advice of four hundred others like himself. Would it not be easier to stand with the majority than to be conspicuously alone? Would it not be easier to tell one lie than to be humiliated in public?

Second, Micaiah was not one of the king's favorites. His position as a prophet was already in jeopardy. Why enrage the king any further? Someday, sometime, Micaiah may find himself in need of the king's support. If he now supported the king in his desires, would not the king be more likely to help him at a later date? As for that, Micaiah was in such trouble now that any negative remarks at this time might cost him his life, or at least banishment.

Third, and above all, Micaiah knew that the king had already made up his mind, that no matter what he would say, the king would ignore him. The case was closed and all Micaiah needed to do was to add his amen.

Those were the conditions that Micaiah faced. Often we find ourselves in the same predicament. It appears that we can save a lot of personal agony by closing our eyes to the truth. It seems that we can spare ourselves by avoiding the commands of truth which spring forth in our hearts. What did Micaiah do? There he stood in that open space before the city gate, in the presence of two kings and four hundred false prophets. Micaiah spoke, saying, "As the LORD liveth, what the LORD saith unto me, that will I speak" (1 Ki 22:14). And Micaiah proceeded to tell the truth, that all Israel would be scattered upon the hills as sheep without a shepherd. What happened? King Ahab went forth to his death. Micaiah went forth to prison. Would it not have been easier for him to lie? At least he could have saved himself.

Jesus knew that those who followed after Him would face this same difficulty. He knew that His followers would be caught in similar situations. Jesus said that men would attempt to persuade us on the one side and on the other. Messengers with secrets of help would come to us as they did to Micaiah. But when man knows the truth in his heart, there are only certain words which he may speak. The follower of Jesus must accept the responsibility which falls upon his shoulders.

St. Paul realized some further implications involved in telling the truth. To be sure, the Bible continually exhorts that a man be truthful. The chronic liar is an offense unto God, but only a cynic speaks the truth at all times. There are some times when the truth need not be spoken, occasions when the truth is of no consequential value in human relationships. There is no value in telling an ugly girl that she is ugly. Telling the truth is more than a principle; it involves personalities and people, human beings created in the image of God. St. Paul admonishes us to speak the truth, but to speak the truth in love (Eph 4:15). Thus, in speaking the truth in love, we are to grow in every way into Him who is the head, into Christ.

Man can only speak the truth by remembering who it is that entitles him to speak, and what it is that we have been

commanded to speak. Remembering that, we will also remember to speak in love, and not to attempt to destroy and
devastate in the name of truth.

Aesop is clever in reminding us what happens to those who
habitually refrain from telling the truth. Experience has
taught us the danger of feeling compelled to always speak
the truth without regard to whom we may be hurting. The
apostle Paul has shown us a better way which leads us to
speak the truth "in love."

A RASH PRAYER ANSWERED

Once upon a time there was a farmer who found a calf missing from his herd. He vowed that he would sacrifice a kid to the gods if he could catch the thief that had stolen his calf. Later as he wandered into the woods he saw a lion devouring his calf. Then in horror he turned his head to heaven and prayed again, "If I promised before to offer up a kid as a sacrifice to discover the thief, now that I have discovered the thief and see him to be a lion, I will offer to sacrifice a bull if I can be delivered safely out of the reach of the lion's claws."

The moral of the story is: "People often pray for things which, when they get them, they discover they really don't want."

It HAS BEEN the problem of man down through the ages in his prayer life to be constantly asking for the right thing, but often in the wrong season. Prayer—the very word itself immediately brings forth the connotation of asking God for something. Its synonymns—request, entreat, implore, beseech—all refer to the petitionary aspect of prayer. This longing of the human heart still represents a valid understanding of our most intimate relationship with God in prayer. But there is the ever present danger of longing for the wrong things.

Plato, in his *Laws,* has an Athenian stranger note the fact that "The desire which a man has that all things, if possible at any rate, things human—may come to pass in accordance with his soul's desire, and having this desire always . . . he cannot help always praying for the fulfillment of it." The problem arises, however, when the son prays to obtain things which the father prays that the son may not obtain. Then seeing the danger of the rash prayers of young fools, Plato notes in classical philosophic terms what once was obvious to the eyes of Aesop, that "the prayer of a fool is full of danger, being likely to end in the opposite of what he desires."

Knowing this danger of petitionary prayer, we are still reminded that Jesus has taught us in all things to make our requests known unto God. Lest there be any question concerning the need of petitionary prayer, Jesus makes this point emphatically clear. When His disciples came to Him, saying, "Lord, teach us to pray," Jesus answered them with a parable.

A certain man was surprised with some company one evening, and in the excitement of getting friends he failed to notice until later that he was without some of the necessary supplies in his kitchen. So he left his home and went to a friend's house even though it was quite late. In fact it was very late; it was midnight. It was dark and all the lights were out and everyone seemed to be in bed. Still he knocked on the door and said, "Friend, lend me three loaves of bread, for company has come to my house and I have nothing to feed them." There was no answer from within, and so he knocked again, and said again, "Friend, lend me three loaves." Then from within he heard a voice saying, "Don't trouble me now. The door is shut and I am in bed, the children are in bed and we cannot get up to give you anything." The man stood still for a moment and then turned to go home. But suddenly he changed his mind and went back to the door and knocked once more, louder than before, so loud that all the dogs in the neighborhood began to bark and howl in apprehensive tones. He persisted and persisted in his demands until at last he saw a light inside. Soon the bars of the door were lifted and as the doors opened he received not only one loaf, but all the bread that he needed. (See Lk 11:5-10.)

Jesus instructs us to use the prayer of petition as a means of filling our lives with those things which we need from the hand of God. He commanded His disciples, knowing of their human needs, that they should pray, "Give us this day our daily bread." We are to ask God not only for the spiritual gifts in this life but also for some of the material needs which we face. Those who hesitate to bother God with their own personal needs are later quite amazed (and sometimes selfishly disappointed) when others who have prayed to God have discovered that their needs have been fulfilled. So Jesus instructs His disciples that they must continually ask and keep on knocking and seeking from the hand of God that which they need in this life.

Man should not be discouraged nor should he be afraid to make his requests known unto God. As fathers we understand this teaching for we too have heard our children as they have come to us with their petitions, their wants and desires. In hearing them, we have come to understand something of their purposes and their hopes. In listening, we have come to understand their reasons and we give them if possible more than that which they ask. What father, if his son asks for a fish will give his son a serpent instead? (Lk 11:11). But there are times when we have had to deny them their requests. What they so urgently and confidently claimed they needed, we as parents knew would ultimately be harmful to them. So often we have gone to God with no doubt in our own thoughts concerning what He should do for us, and in our petitions we let God know exactly what we feel we need. At times we are like Aesop's fool, for without realizing it we are praying for our own destruction.

It is here that Christ's teaching on prayer becomes difficult to understand. We see that His instruction bears more than one command. It can be understood from different vantage points. It is a many-faceted teaching, and its brilliance is heightened as we turn it in the light of our experience and understanding. To be sure, Christ has taught us to pray without ceasing. He has taught us to keep seeking, asking, and knocking. But there is the other side of His teaching which comes not so much from what He said as by what He did. That night when Christ went out after the Last Supper to the Mount of Olives, He prayed, "Father, if Thou art willing, remove this cup from Me. Yet not My will, but Thine be done" (Lk 22:42, NASB). Here Christ teaches us that there will come a time when we must put aside our persistent asking and seeking, when we must acknowledge the will of God for our own lives and yield ourselves totally to Him. Even little children understand (if not from words, at least from experience) that there comes a time when they should no longer beg and plead for something which obviously and evidently they should not have. Though their answer was not direct, they understood the intent and will of their fathers. Therefore, they learn in time to acquiesce.

It was something of this nature that the apostle Paul tried to explain to the members of the early Corinthian church. He reminded them of the thorn which he had in the flesh which he considered to be a messenger of Satan continually harassing him. Paul said that he prayed to God for deliverance from this pain. Paul was asking God to free him from the one thing that seemed to deter him in his attempts to serve God. It was a most justifiable prayer, a prayer which logic would lead us to believe ought to have been answered immediately by God. To the contrary, Paul informs us that he sought God's healing three times, and he was not healed. After this time Paul desisted from praying for deliverance in this matter. He learned that God's power was going to be made manifest in spite of his human weakness, and that the weakness was in part the very cause which would effect the power of God. Paul observed then what he never would have been able to understand if he had been healed, that "for the sake of Christ I am content with weakness, insults, hardships, persecutions and calamities. For when I am weak, then I am strong" (2 Co 12:10).

The apostle Paul had learned something of what Martin Luther referred to as "abandoned prayers." There are prayers which we at one time did present to God in a sense of urgency and despair and importunity. In time we have learned that we were not as wise as we once thought, and in accepting God's verdict in answer to our lives, we learned to let the matter fall. Often we saw with some embarrassment at a later date that the very thing which we prayed for would have been the cause of our future despair!

All the wisdom of the world has not yet enlightened us to that clear understanding whereby we can discern which prayers should be carried forth endlessly to the mercy seat of God, and what prayers should be abandoned to His will. But let us at least this day understand that when our own petitions are not answered as we desire, we may, with the apostle Paul, discover that our prayers may be full of danger to ourselves, being likely at times to end in the opposite of what we once desired.

GO TO THE ANT, THOU
SLUGGARD

Once upon a time an ant spent its whole summer gathering grains of wheat and barley to store for the winter. A beetle which watched the ant suggested that maybe the ant ought to take a vacation in the summer and rest from all its labors. The ant said nothing.

But when winter came, the beetle had no food. Famished with hunger the beetle came to the ant begging for some food to eat. The ant said, "You should have worked during the summer instead of laughing at me. If you had worked then, you would not be short of food now."

The moral of the story is: "A man should take thought for the morrow in a time of abundance so that he might not be in distress in a time of need."

FROM THE EARLIEST TIMES, the Hebrews regarded work as a divine command from which no human was exempted. We read in the Ten Commandments, "Six days shalt thou labour and do all thy work" (Ex 20:9). It was expected that men would live and labor. It was the conviction of the Hebrews that idleness would be ruinous. Thus when we meet Saul as he is about to be chosen king of Israel, we see him as a man coming from his calling in the fields (1 Sa 11:5). The fact that he walked behind his oxen did not tarnish his royal image. Work was seen as a blessing and not as a curse laid upon man for his sins, and Saul was ennobled through his travail. Even Adam was instructed to replenish the earth and subdue it and have dominion over it (Gen 1:28). He was to dress and keep the garden of Eden (Gen 2:15), and work was to become the natural functioning of man in the world. It was not surprising that the Old Testament sage should enjoin the populace, saying "Go to the ant, thou sluggard; consider her ways, and be wise" (Pr 6:6).

In the New Testament, the biblical understanding of work is fulfilled by Christ Himself who became a carpenter, a craftsman who accepted work as a law of God for human living. The fact of life was thus simply stated, that unless a man chose to exploit his fellowmen, he had to work in order to live. Although we thank the apostle Paul for his clarity of language, we must admit that he was not the first to state that "If anyone will not work, neither let him eat" (2 Th 3:10, NASB). Paul knew that there were some members of the church in Thessalonica who were refusing to work, who preferred to have their fellow Christians labor for them. Paul was especially concerned in this situation. Even though he knew that he had the legal right to receive pay for his preaching, he gave up this privilege in order to better enforce his example and his teaching of the necessity of labor. For the sake of the converts, he once again bore witness to the necessity of disciplined labor and his work was the double labor of physical as well as mental activity. Thus his body as well as his mind was in constant readiness for the arduous tasks ahead. Because of the discipline of his preparation, he was able to meet the demands of every occasion in every season. Therefore Paul was able to write without any sense of false modesty, "For you yourselves know how you ought to imitate us; we were not idle when we were with you" (2 Th 3:7, RSV).

How times have changed! Though our situation is the same as that of the early members of the church in Thessalonica, we imitate neither the ant nor the apostle Paul. Rather than choosing the biblical roads of discipline, we have entered the easier paths of the pleasures of prosperity. We are living in a day when there is a widespread desire for that state of passivity which we wrongly associate with the Garden of Eden. We search for a life where work is a thing of the past and where labor is merely a matter of pressing buttons—buttons that drive our automobiles, whose dashboards are cluttered with other buttons that operate windows, radios, and the temperature; buttons in our homes that have the power to produce music, speeches, and ball games, and to command the great events of the world that appear right before our eyes; buttons that energize machines which wash our clothes, and then dry them; cook our meals and then wash our dishes. Indeed, we live in a push-button paradise here on earth far greater than any Garden of Eden known to Adam.

It is no wonder that in our society today, a young man's dream is to be able to live without working. But let us be well reminded that what is a dream to a young man is often a nightmare to his father. For though a little leisure is a wonderful thing, a continuing vacation from work, the final retirement from human labor, is a fearful thing unless work is seen as a part of our human existence which leads us into some thought and preparation for the morrow. Work which gives some meaning for today must hold some purpose for tomorrow.

Unlike the ant, man's work must have a purpose beyond that of productivity and self-preservation. Our work must be seen as a creative rather than a consuming experience. We must be able to see in what appears to be daily drudgery some season of abundance for Christ's sake. It is this obligation—to be a part of God's total plan for humanity— which gives meaning and direction to our work. Unlike the ant who carries food all summer to store for the winter, our human labor becomes meaningful only and in so far as we can see the greater purpose of God for all mankind, and therein our labor takes its form. Our reaction then to our labor will not be one of hostility seeking release from enforced duties; nor will it be one of necessity, feeling that we do not deserve to eat lest we labor; but our attitude toward work will then be that of cheerful satisfaction in being able to participate in God's total plan for the whole world of which we are an integral part. So we are instructed to give ourselves, body and soul, to all the tasks which confront us, not with the hope of someday being at rest from our labors but instead with the hope of someday hearing in the midst of our labors, "Well done, thou good and faithful servant."

FAMILIARITY BREEDS CONTEMPT

Once upon a time when a man first saw a camel, he was terrified by its huge size and he ran away. But in the days that followed he learned that the camel was a gentle beast and he soon developed courage enough to approach it. Little by little he came to realize that the camel was incapable of showing anger. Then the man learned to despise the camel and he put a bridle on it and let his children drive it around.

The moral of the story is: "Many formidable things lose their terror when we become accustomed to them."

NOTHING IN THIS WORLD is as demoralizing, disabling, and devitalizing as being taken for granted. From puppy love to pure love, from adolescence to maturity, there is no plan as diabolically insidious as this, that one person should take another for granted. The advice-to-the-lovelorn columns in daily newspapers are filled with the tearful cries of those lovers who feel that they are being abused simply because they feel that they are being taken for granted. Countless souls who once felt that close proximity yielded a certain right of propriety later cried out in powerless pleas that now, being used to a proprietous relationship, they feel they are being treated with a certain degree of contempt. In human relations there is always the need to demonstrate that we are not taking one another for granted. But the difficulties arise in our attempts to demonstrate a degree of personal concern and affection. The traditionally accepted form in our American way of life is by the presentation of an unexpected and unmerited gift. The husband who surprisingly brings home a bouquet of flowers is in some way trying to express to his wife that he does not take her for granted. Furthermore, he is offering something of his own resources to show that he acknowledges the source and the end of his human concern. These small tokens of love which husbands and wives affectionately exchange are visible and outward signs of the fact that they have not taken each other for granted.

The Israelites were unsurpassed in the area of giving visible tokens of dedication. If we were to add up all the sacrifices and offerings presented by any typical family of the Old Testament period, we would soon discover that a large portion of their earthly substance was consecrated to religious uses. In our day and age when we feel that we are being overly taxed in our time and substance for the life of the church, we might do well to examine the amount of time and substance our forefathers dedicated to religious service. Though we may criticize the Jews for their vacillating sense of obedience, for their constant violation of God's commandments, and perhaps even improper motives, we must remind ourselves that at least they did not withhold their material goods from the Lord.

When Moses heard the voice of God in the burning bush, he turned aside to see the great sight. But God said to Moses, "Draw not nigh hither: put off thy shoes from off thy feet, for the place whereon thou standest is holy ground" (Ex 3:5). Moses, in a great sense of fearful reverence, did as he was commanded. Later, Joshua coming into the new and promised land stood in wonder before that city of Jericho when a man appeared to him with his sword drawn. Falling on his face Joshua asked, "What does my Lord bid his servant?" And the commander of the Lord's army replied, "Put off your shoes from your feet; for the place where you stand is holy." And Joshua did so (Jos 5:14-15). In the presence of the Lord his God, Joshua stood in fear and trembling, and that great mystery of the otherness of God which separates the Creator from the creature became evident once again.

Throughout the pages of the Old Testament, we see men approaching God with fearful reverence while entering into the temple to worship Him. And only a few were allowed into that sanctuary in which His presence dwelt. But in turning to the pages of the New Testament, we read that when Jesus Christ appeared, He entered once and for all into that holy place, taking not the blood of goats and calves, but His own blood, thus securing for us an eternal salvation (Heb 9:12).

The Old Testament's understanding of man's relationship with God has changed. No longer do we need to depend on an intermediary who would annually enter into the holy of holies in the tabernacle. Now man is able through Jesus Christ to know God in a firsthand manner. But the danger also arises that in this firsthand relationship, man may, in his sense of familiarity, lose some sense of his reverence and awe of God. Furthermore, since in Jesus Christ that separation between Creator and creature has been bridged, and seeing that Christ has already made the perfect sacrifice for him, man may now lose some of his sense of the need for his own life being a continual sacrifice unto God. Man now stands in danger of losing his reverence for the holiness of God. What a strange paradox of life it is, that God, who has given us freedom of will, takes no man for granted. To demonstrate His love for us, He gave us the perfect sacrifice of love in Jesus Christ, only to realize that we, having received this sacrifice of love, are now tempted in our personal relationship with Jesus Christ to forsake our sacrifices and take His love for granted.

In this modern world we have seen and heard so much of young lovers whose close relationship has given them a false sense of propriety. Similarly, Christians are in danger of falling into a false sense of propriety in their close relationship with a God who so loved the world that He gave His only begotten Son. Let us take care, or the formidable things of God will lose their awesome and proper holiness when we get used to them.

PRIDE WILL HAVE A FALL

Once upon a time the mice were at war with the weasels. It seemed that the mice were always getting the worst of it, so the mice held a meeting and they decided their constant defeat was due to a lack of strong leadership. They chose some of their number to become their leaders and made them generals. These chosen mice, being proud of their new distinction, wanted to separate themselves from the other mice so they made horns and fixed them on their heads so that they would be conspicuous.

At the time of the next battle the mice were again defeated by the weasels and the mice turned to take flight to safety. They all got safely into their holes except the generals, who were unable to enter because of the size of their horns. They were caught and devoured by the weasels.

The moral of the story is: "Vainglory is often the cause of our misfortunes."

THERE ARE DANGERS in carrying one's head too high, both in relation to other men and in relation to God. Contention in life comes when a person begins to grow proud in himself and then, fearful of his own acclaimed status, he arrogantly attempts to affirm his worth by throwing his head higher than it ought to be and resenting any threat to his self-imposed position. In carrying the head high, man attempts to distinguish himself by saying to the world, "Look how smart, how rich, or how important I am." When the world does look, it sees not the glory which our own imaginative minds have conjectured. Instead it often sees all the faults and shortcomings which we have overlooked in ourselves in our desire to appear greater than we are. Consequently, as Shakespeare's Agamemnon said once to Ajax the Grecian commander:

> He that is proud eats up himself; pride is his own glass, his own trumpet, his own chronicle; and whatever praises itself but in the deed devours the deed in the praise.

Our sin of pride is not a singular situation. The Bible is replete with accounts of human strivings and human failings. Unfortunately, even the oft-quoted proverb "Pride goeth before destruction, and an haughty spirit before a fall" (Pr 16:18) failed to deter the men of old (as well as the men today) from walking the foolish pathways of pride.

Perhaps the most pitiable Old Testament account of the peril of pride is that of the two sons of Isaac who, being of different natures, were pitted against each other in sibling rivalry. Their youthful quarreling was nurtured into adult animosity, and at last Jacob's ultimate deception in gaining Esau's inheritance caused the two brothers to part company. Jacob went to live in the land of Haran and Esau departed to dwell in the land of Edom. History records that these two brothers became the heads of the tribes of Edom and Israel, nations which lived in bitter enmity with each other. Each was proud of its own historical past, and each refused to acknowledge the worth of the other.

The Israelites based their pride largely on the fact that they were chosen as the tribe for the fulfillment of the Messianic future. The Edomites, on the other hand, based their pride not in the future, but in the strength and power they possessed over the present. The Edomites, living in the rocky crags of Mount Seir, felt that they were invulnerable to attack from without and therefore secure and safe forever. The Israelites, presuming that they were God's chosen people, were proud also of their invulnerability because of the power of their God. In time Israel fell, and the Edomites, safe and secure in their rocky cliffs, laughed in scornful pride at their fallen brothers. In anger and hurt pride the prophet Obadiah cried out to the children of Edom, "The pride of thine heart hath deceived thee, thou that dwellest in the clefts of the rock, whose habitation is high; that saith in his heart, Who shall bring me down to the ground? . . . I bring thee down, saith the LORD" (Ob 3-4). In time they did fall, and great was the destruction of the children of Edom.

In the New Testament, Jesus seems constantly concerned lest His followers fall victim to the perils of pride. He knew very well that pride was one of the besetting sins of the Pharisees and that they loved to seek places of prominence among men. One Sabbath day, when He had been invited to dine at the house of a ruler who was also a Pharisee, Jesus could not resist telling a parable. When He noted how the guests had chosen their places of honor at the table, He told them the story of a man who, in his own self-established pride, took a place of greater importance at a banquet table than he deserved. Jesus then left to our imagination the embarrassment of this man when the host came to him and asked him to move down to a lesser place to make room for another more important guest. Therefore Jesus said, "When you are invited to a feast, sit in the lowest place so that when your host comes, he may say, 'Go up higher.' Then you will be honored in the presence of those who sit at the table. For everyone who exalts himself will be humbled and he who humbles himself will be exalted" (see Lk 14:1-11). Jesus is showing that humility is the antithesis of pride. The humble man recognizes his creatureliness, his dependence upon God and upon others. This does not by any means indicate that he should think of himself as being less worthy than others. Instead it means that he understands that the source of his worth is through the grace of God and not through himself, nor is it dependent on the opinions of others.

On this particular subject, it appears that Jesus felt that we need more than one lesson. To doubly instruct us, He told a different parable of pride, this time the story of two men who went up into the temple to pray. One was a Pharisee and the other a tax collector. The Pharisee stood and prayed aloud about himself, saying, "God, I thank thee that I am not like other men, extortioners, unjust, adulterers, or even like this publican." But the publican standing far off would not even do as much as raise his eyes to heaven. Instead, he beat his breast and said, "God, be merciful to me a sinner." Jesus said of the publican, "I tell you, this man went back to his house justified. For everyone who exalts himself shall be humbled, but he who humbles himself shall be exalted." (See Lk 18:10-14.)

Strange indeed—Jesus, the only One who has any reason

for pride, should have been so emphatic once upon a time, yes, even twice upon a time, to have stated that, "Everyone who exalts himself shall be humbled, but he who humbles himself shall be exalted."